Business Architecture

Landmark Books by Meghan-Kiffer Press

DOT.CLOUD
THE 21ST CENTURY BUSINESS PLATFORM
BUILT ON CLOUD COMPUTING

ENTERPRISE CLOUD COMPUTING
A STRATEGY GUIDE FOR BUSINESS AND TECHNOLOGY LEADERS

EXTREME COMPETITION
INNOVATION AND THE GREAT 21ST CENTURY
BUSINESS REFORMATION

BUSINESS PROCESS MANAGEMENT
THE THIRD WAVE

MASTERING THE UNPREDICTABLE
HOW ADAPTIVE CASE MANAGEMENT WILL REVOLUTIONIZE
THE WAY THAT KNOWLEDGE WORKERS GET THINGS DONE

POWER IN TE CLOUD
USING CLOUD COMPUTING
TO BUILD INFORMATION SYSTEMS AT THE EDGE OF CHAOS

IT DOESN'T MATTER:
BUSINESS PROCESSES DO

THE REAL-TIME ENTERPRISE
COMPETING ON TIME

THE DEATH OF 'E' AND
THE BIRTH OF THE REAL NEW ECONOMY

ENTERPRISE E-COMMERCE

THE BLUEPRINT FOR BUSINESS OBJECTS

THE INSIDERS' GUIDE TO BPM
7 STEPS TO PROCESS MASTERY

Meghan-Kiffer Press
www.mkpress.com
Innovation at the Intersection of Business and Technology

Business Architecture

The Art and Practice of
Business Transformation

William Ulrich
Neal McWhorter

Meghan-Kiffer Press
Tampa, Florida, USA, www.mkpress.com
Advanced Business-Technology Books for Competitive Advantage

Publisher's Cataloging-in-Publication Data

Ulrich, William.
 Business Architecture / William Ulrich, Neal McWhorter, - 1st ed.
  p. cm.
  Includes index.
  ISBN 978-0929652-15-3 (cloth : alk. paper)

  1. Organizational effectiveness 2. Strategic Planning. 3. Complex organizations. 4. Organizational change. 5. Management. 6. Complex adaptive systems. 7. Information resources management. I. Ulrich, William. II. McWhorter, Neal. III. Title

HD58.87.U548 2011   2010939678
658.4'063–dc21   CIP

Limited distribution edition first published November, 2010 © 2010.
Published by Meghan-Kiffer Press
 310 East Fern Street — Suite G
 Tampa, FL 33604 USA

Company and product names mentioned herein are the trademarks or registered trademarks of their respective owners.

Meghan-Kiffer books are available at special quantity discounts for corporate education and training use. For more information write Special Sales, Meghan-Kiffer Press, Suite G, 310 East Fern Street, Tampa, Florida 33604 or email orders@mkpress.com

Meghan-Kiffer Press
Tampa, Florida, USA
Publishers of Advanced Business-Technology Books for Competitive Advantage

Printed in the United States of America.   SAN 249-7980
MK Printing 10 9 8 7 6 5 4 3 2 1

This book is dedicated to the business architects
of 21st century corporations.

Table of Contents

YOUR PLAN OF ACTION

PREFACE

INTRODUCTION 19

ONE
WHY BUSINESS ARCHITECTURE MATTERS 25

AN EXECUTIVE PERSPECTIVE: THE TITANIC STORY 27
A PRACTITIONER'S PERSPECTIVE:
   MAN THE LIFEBOATS OR REARRANGE THE DECK CHAIRS 31
SORTING THROUGH THE MAZE OF REDUNDANT, FRAGMENTED
   BUSINESS INFRASTRUCTURES 33
ENDING THE CYCLE OF FAILED MULTI-YEAR INITIATIVES 37
BUSINESS ARCHITECTURE HELPS REFOCUS STRATEGIC INVESTMENTS 39
STOP RECREATING THE WHEEL ON EVERY INITIATIVE 42
PRIMITIVE DEPLOYMENTS OF BUSINESS ARCHITECTURE 44
CAPTURING THE ESSENCE OF THE BUSINESS
   IN BUSINESS ARCHITECTURE 45
VISUALIZING THE BUSINESS THROUGH BUSINESS ARCHITECTURE 49
MAPPING THE VIRTUAL ENTERPRISE 53
BUSINESS ARCHITECTURE, IT ARCHITECTURE AND
   ENTERPRISE ARCHITECTURE 55
CURRENT STATE VS. FUTURE STATE BUSINESS ARCHITECTURE 56
A FRAMEWORK FOR BUSINESS ARCHITECTURE 57
WHAT'S NEXT? 58

TWO
THE TRANSPARENT ENTERPRISE 61

THE NEED FOR VISIBILITY 63
WHEN VISIBILITY BREAKS DOWN:
   THE HYATT REGENCY CROWN CENTER DISASTER 65
EXISTING LEVELS OF TRANSPARENCY ARE NOT ENOUGH 67
A DIFFERENT KIND OF TRANSPARENCY 70
THE BUSINESS ARCHITECTURE DASHBOARD 73
BEHIND THE DASHBOARD:
   THE BUSINESS ARTIFACT KNOWLEDGEBASE 76
PURSUING BUSINESS AIMS: APPLYING THE KNOWLEDGEBASE 78
EXERCISING THE BUSINESS ARCHITECTURE DASHBOARD 81
BEYOND THE DASHBOARD:

COMMON BUSINESS ARCHITECTURE VISUALIZATIONS 83
SHIFTING FROM OPERATIONAL TO STRATEGIC DASHBOARDS...............87

THREE
BUILDING THE BUSINESS ARCHITECTURE TEAM 89

THE BUSINESS ARCHITECT..91
THE BUSINESS ARCHITECT VS. THE BUSINESS ANALYST 95
BUSINESS ARCHITECTURE CENTER OF EXCELLENCE..............................96
BUSINESS ARCHITECTURE COE ACCOUNTABILITY & OWNERSHIP 97
COMMONLY APPLIED BUSINESS ARCHITECTURE
ORGANIZING CONCEPTS.. 100
IDEAL BUSINESS ARCHITECTURE ORGANIZATIONAL STRUCTURE 104
THE AGILE BUSINESS ARCHITECTURE ENGAGEMENT MODEL........... 107
THE MULTI-DIVISIONAL COE ORGANIZATIONAL STRUCTURE.......... 109
COLLABORATIVE GOVERNANCE:
TEAMING WITH BUSINESS UNITS, IT & EXTERNAL ENTITIES............ 114

FOUR
BUSINESS ARCHITECTURE AND
IT ARCHITECTURE ALIGNMENT...121

A BUSINESS-DRIVEN APPROACH TO IT ARCHITECTURE STRATEGY.... 123
ALIGNING BUSINESS AND IT STRATEGY
VIA BUSINESS ARCHITECTURE 124
THE BUSINESS - IT COMMUNICATION & LANGUAGE GAP................... 127
REFOCUSING THE ENTERPRISE ON BUSINESS-DRIVEN IT STRATEGY. 128
ESTABLISHING A BUSINESS-DRIVEN TRANSFORMATION STRATEGY ... 131
A QUICK PRIMER ON IT ARCHITECTURE.. 133
VISUALIZING IT ARCHITECTURE FROM A BUSINESS PERSPECTIVE 136
SYNCHRONIZED, BUSINESS-DRIVEN BUSINESS AND IT ALIGNMENT.. 144
ARCHITECTURE-DRIVEN MODERNIZATION &
BUSINESS TRANSFORMATION... 154
BUSINESS AND IT ARCHITECTURE ALIGNMENT SUMMARIZATION 159

FIVE
BUSINESS ARCHITECTURE IN PRACTICE 161

A PARABLE.. 163
WHAT MAKES A PROBLEM PROBLEMATIC? 164
ASPECTS OF A BUSINESS ARCHITECTURE.. 165
CAPABILITY-BASED ANALYSIS & INVESTMENT 166
MERGER & ACQUISITION PLANNING & DEPLOYMENT 168
INFRASTRUCTURE INVESTMENT ANALYSIS.. 174
SHIFT TO CUSTOMER CENTRICITY 180

New Product and Service Rollout 181
New Business Line Introduction 182
Streamlining the Supply Chain 184
Outsourcing a Business Capability 185
Divesting a Line of Business 186
Change Management 187
Regulatory Compliance 188
Operational Cost Reduction 189
Globalization 191
Addressing Business Transformation 191

SIX
GETTING STARTED WITH BUSINESS ARCHITECTURE.......193

Business Architecture Value Proposition 195
Engagement Models and Deployment Teams............................. 199
Roadmap Deployment 203
Care and Feeding of
    the Business Architecture Knowledgebase 210
Technology Tool Guidelines for Business Architecture...... 213
Seven Building Blocks of Business Architecture 216

INDEX 221

ABOUT THE AUTHORS.. 226

Your Plan of Action

Visualizing a business through architectural disciplines is not entirely new. Creating a business friendly framework that allows business professionals to visualize and transform organizations, however, is a groundbreaking achievement. We don't want you to just read this book, we want you to act on it. This and the following pages are for you to make some notes, to write down the transformational action items for your organization.

Preface

Companies are investing in business architecture and their efforts are paying off.

A major insurance company has taken significant strides toward shifting its business model from being product line centric to customer-centric. The result? Customer attrition has fallen off.

Other organizations are leveraging business architecture to re-evaluate investment priorities, launch cross-product line initiatives, streamline and consolidate business units, address regulatory challenges and reposition themselves to compete on a global level.

Using business architecture, businesses can make better, more informed decisions and deliver bottom line value as a result of those decisions.

Organizations have grown so complex in recent years that it is difficult to visualize or understand how all of the parts fit together. Every business unit has its own set of funded initiatives and it is difficult to see how or even if these initiatives align to a common business strategy.

At the same time, executives want to reshape organizations to be more competitive and more customer-centric as quickly and as efficiently as possible. This requires horizontal solutions, where executives across business units view issues and solutions from a shared, enterprise-wide perspective.

We wrote this book to share the value of business architecture with the target audience that can benefit the most – business executives, managers and professionals. Business architecture helps these individuals make and implement decisions more effectively by instilling much needed transparency into the decision making process.

The benefits of business architecture are spreading as more organizations embrace this important discipline. The most important aspect of business architecture, however, is often overlooked – enabling business executives, managers and professionals to take ownership and drive enterprise transformation, a role that has oftentimes been delegated by default to IT.

William Ulrich
Neal McWhorter
2011

INTRODUCTION

Digitization represents a revolution that may be the greatest opportunity for growth that our company has ever seen.
—GE, Key Growth Initiatives 2002.

Business architecture is a business discipline that is owned by the business, for the business. Business architecture is not about technology, but it does allow business to reclaim leadership and leverage when it comes to transforming the business. This concept is essential in an age when solutions to complex business challenges are often relegated down to two topics: Services-Oriented Architecture (SOA) and Cloud Computing. These IT-specific disciplines are a means to an end – not an end in and of themselves. In addition, these IT related terms have little place in discussions on business strategy and business transformation.

Business architecture's value is being recognized on a wide range of initiatives including merger and acquisition planning and deployment, new product rollout, globalization, operational streamlining, regulatory compliance management, outsourcing analysis, customer management and the shift to customer centricity. The value of business architecture can be summarized into three major categories: root cause analysis, planning visibility and the ability to create and drive transformation roadmaps.

Root cause analysis is a key value proposition for business architecture, providing refreshing transparency into complex business challenges that cross business unit or even organizational boundaries. Understanding the root causes behind issues such as customer attrition, competitive losses or missed business opportunities is half the battle when it comes to establishing viable, robust solutions. Speculation in management meetings tends to run discussions in circles, with everyone proposing piecemeal solutions for poorly articulated problems. These discussions can go on for weeks or months, finally ending by throwing money at an assortment of high cost, multi-year initiatives in the hopes that they solve the problem.

Business architecture's ability to bring visibility to impact analysis and change management is essential in deciphering action plans and roadmaps. Business architecture allows planning teams and executive committees to build strategies with a clear view of horizontal business impacts. There are already too many silo-based projects in the works across various business units, each driven by executives who see a piece of the problem and a slice of the solution. The collective impacts of these efforts, many of which run into conflict with each other, are beyond the line of sight of the executive committees responsible for governing them. Business architecture sheds light on the horizontal and vertical impacts of cross-functional initiatives, allowing executives to align them in a way that is in line with the enterprise strategy as a whole.

For example, a financial institution had launched multiple "lean" value stream projects to streamline processes within a number of divisions. Each project was being driven by individual business unit and product line executives. The business benefits of these investment activities on an individual basis made perfect sense, but when viewed at an enterprise level they introduced extreme risk into the organization. Several of the value stream lean projects clashed in ways that were suboptimal from the perspective of the whole. In addition, these projects would collectively and individually create significant downstream problems from an IT transformation perspective. A business architecture assessment, which looked at the value stream projects and related impacts from an enterprise perspective, brought these risks to light and allowed the executive steering committee to instill the governance and direction required to align these projects and gain more significant benefits in the long run.

Our third category involves business's ability drive enterprise transformation from a business perspective. Business architecture empowers the business to play a key role in driving coherent business and IT transformation strategies and roadmaps – from a business perspective. The Standish Group found that out of the annual $364 billion spent on IT projects, $160 billion of those investments was considered waste.

With this track record and so much pressure being brought to bear on businesses to reinvent themselves along more efficient, globally focused and customer-centric lines, organizations cannot afford to squander major capital investments. This is not an indictment of IT but rather a call to action for business executives to take ownership of business architecture and related business transformation strategies. The decisions that are made today can make or break organizations going forward into a complex, uncertain future.

When it comes down to it, the value proposition for business architecture is as simple as this. Business architecture sheds light on complex challenges and solutions by introducing a degree of visibility into the situation that did not exist in the past. In doing so, strategic decision and investments can be made with more confidence, deliver more effective results and do so with less investment than what is currently being spent on major initiatives today. We hope that this book on business architecture becomes a staple in business planning and transformation efforts as your organization moves forward into the complex, challenging world ahead.

How We Organized this Book

We organized this book into six chapters for ease of reading and ease of reference. We took a case study oriented approach and followed a particular business scenario across several of the chapters to highlight the practical application of business architecture. Chapter 1 provides an introduction to business architecture and the case for business architecture. Citing various industry case study scenarios and work in progress, we established a business case for business architecture based on a history of successes and failures as well as the challenges that lie ahead.

Chapter 2 is called the "Transparent Enterprise" and discusses the different viewpoints brought to bear by business architecture. Drawing analogies to construction failures resulting from a lack of visibility, highlights similar risks facing businesses today when they lack visibility into their business and related transformation efforts. We also discuss how business architecture visibility does not focus on financial performance of the business but rather on the construction, makeup and evolution of the enterprise as a whole.

Chapter 2 also includes examples of the "blueprints" or viewpoints embodied within business architecture including dashboards, the capability map, organizational models and business cross-reference maps. Finally, we introduce the concept of the business architecture framework as a way of establishing and leveraging your business architecture knowledgebase and related business viewpoints that collectively comprise the essence of the business architecture.

Chapter 3 discusses how to establish the business architecture team. We walk through a number of different team building and rollout scenarios based on experiences at a number of companies. We also discuss the role of the business architect within the context of the business unit and the business architecture center of excellence. In addition, we explore the pluses and minuses of various approaches for setting up and governing business architecture.

Chapter 4 delves into the topic of business architecture and IT architecture alignment. While business architecture is not about IT, business transformation requires the synchronized evolution of IT architecture. Recognizing this fact, Chapter 4 discusses the ramifications of business transformation on IT architecture, which include the applications and information structures organizations rely on to survive and thrive. The business-driven focus of this discussion sheds new light on how organizations can evolve complex IT architectures in ways that deliver value to the business early and on an ongoing basis.

Chapter 5 is called "Business Architecture in Practice" and

expands upon many of the business architecture scenarios that were introduced in prior discussions. These scenarios address what we consider to be the obvious challenges where business architecture can make an impact. Scenarios include merger and acquisition analysis, infrastructure investment analysis, operational cost containment, new product and service rollout, regulatory management and several other common scenarios.

Chapter 6 ties together a number of the previous topics. In this chapter, we expand upon the value proposition, discussing ways to position and fund business architecture initiatives. We also expand upon the Chapter 3 topic of team building with a discussion of business architecture engagement models, which provides readers with ideas on how to organize business architecture assessment, planning and roadmap deployment – including business and IT engagement. We also offer additional insights into setting up and managing the business architecture "knowledgebase" where information about the business is collected and housed.

Chapter 6 also provides an overview of technology tool requirements for business architecture. Lastly, we close out our discussions by leaving readers with the "seven building blocks of business architecture," which accommodates the concept of staged maturation of the business architecture deployment process.

Who Should Read This Book

There are a number of target audiences for this book but the book is specifically targeted at business executives and managers who are struggling with many of the challenges we discuss throughout the text. Another prime target of this book is the business architect who can use this book as a guide for establishing and practicing business architecture.

Business analysts should also consider this book as a "must read" because it provides insights into new ways to view business requirements and business and IT transformation. Business process analysts should also find significant value in a number of the chapters as there are inherent business process governance concepts within business architecture that allow organizations to increase the overall benefits of business process modeling within a much larger context.

Another category of reader who would benefit from this book is the enterprise architect and IT architect. Specifically, data and application architects within IT will find the business and IT architecture alignment discussions of great value because they provide them with the insights needed to improve the value of their respective roles. IT executives and managers will also gain significant value from the book, particularly because it positions business and IT alignment from a business perspective.

One last group of readers involves the external services provider and technology tool provider. There are a number of consulting disciplines that enter the realm of business architecture such as creating lean value streams. While this work is of value, creating lean value streams under the auspices of the business architecture offers the visibility and transparency required to ensure that these efforts are well conceived and effectively governed.

One

Why Business Architecture Matters

The art of simplicity is a puzzle of complexity.
—Doug Horton

You find yourself in an executive session with several frustrated senior vice presidents. The company has been losing market share, your chief competitor, an agile newcomer, has just passed you by and you are now ranked third in an industry you used to dominate. Your senior executives want to know what is at the core of these losses and, more importantly, what action they can take to regain the company's competitive position. You were invited to the meeting because you were recently put in charge of the company's business architecture team. Management wants options as to how to address these issues – and they are looking for you to provide them.

As you leave the meeting, ideas are racing through your head. How can your team help determine the root cause of the customer losses, communicate this message to management without going into lengthy detail and recommend a viable course of action that can be implemented enterprise-wide? The only thing you are sure of at this point is that you need to come back with answers – in short order. Welcome to the world of business architecture.

An Executive Perspective: The Titanic story

As organizations and industries grow increasingly complex, the need to respond rapidly to evermore pressing issues has grown exponentially, even as enterprise agility has suffered. One thing that corporations and government entities have in common is the need to quickly troubleshoot issues, craft strategies and deploy solutions based on a shared understanding of the root cause of the problem. This last point is where one of the greatest challenges emerges. Most enterprises lack a well articulated, commonly agreed upon view of their enterprise and this can stymie situation analysis, cripple decision making and undermine solution deployments.

In the movie *Titanic* (the 1998 version), rapid diagnosis and action were required. After Titanic hit the iceberg, the Captain and his first officers gathered on deck as the Titanic's architect unrolled a blueprint of the ship. All eyes focused on the skeletal structure of the massive, "unsinkable" ship as it was unfurled before them. As the architect pointed out the seam that had been torn open along the starboard side of the hull, everyone looking over the architect's shoulder knew it was serious. It took only seconds for the Captain to determine a course of action – abandon ship. The ship's blueprint, shown in Figure 1.1, provided the Captain and his officers with an easily understood, common frame of reference.

Figure 1.1: Ship's Blueprint

If only business decisions could be made this quickly and with such resolve. Most of the time, however, executives cannot get to the root cause of an issue and management is forced to fund multiple initiatives, hoping one of them will address the underlying problem. In other cases, decisions are not made at all because management is trapped in a series of meetings, rehashing the cause and effect of key issues.

A worst case scenario leads to blind decisions to invest tens of millions of dollars in technology with the vague promise that a new set of systems will solve your business problems. In each of these scenarios, the reason behind the indecision, revolving door meetings and blind investments in new technology is the inability to articulate the root cause and required response to a wide range of issues with bottom line consequences.

Executives lack a formal blueprint of the enterprise – a blueprint that facilitates rapid situation analysis, exposes the root cause of critical issues and allows solutions to present themselves in the clear light of day. These blueprints are not in anyone's head.

Even if they were, there is no vehicle in place for exposing various business viewpoints that can serve as the basis for reasoning, planning and deployment. Organizations have grown too complex for any individual or group of individuals to fully understand the cause and effects of complex issues and articulate the full scope, impacts and risks of proposed solutions – without a blueprint of the business.

Worse yet, when decisions are made and communicated through layers of management and across business units, the ability of deployment teams to zoom in on increasingly granular views of issues and solutions is blurred and often off target. Not only is there no high-level blueprint for executive analysis and decision making, there is no underlying blueprint to facilitate detailed planning and execution of these decisions.

Even when teams are successful in understanding and implementing a given project, there are typically several other initiatives aimed at addressing the same issue and that deliver conflicting results. In some cases, projects work at cross purposes with other projects in unrelated parts of the enterprise. Redundant functionality and organizational structures are a reality in today's enterprise. Studies show, for example, that redundancy is rampant across organizations. An IBM research project conducted across a series of financial institutions found that 60-80% of a given set of functionality can be found in other parts of the enterprise. [1]

Redundancy, while useful and even planned in some cases,

can result in wasted resources, lost opportunities and inconsistency in dealing with customers and the market in general if it is unplanned and left unchecked. When this occurs within a company that has undergone a merger or acquisition, or that has multiple product lines servicing an overlapping customer base, redundancy becomes even more detrimental to management's ability to apply scarce funding to a positive effect on the bottom line.

One result of inherent enterprise complexity and redundancy is that funding major initiatives has become much more difficult as multi-year projects chew up vast resources while other requirements remain undiagnosed and unfunded. Consider the case where a group of senior portfolio managers were seeking to divvy up discretionary funds within an annual budget allocation. As each portfolio manager made his or her case to the others, it was clear that they were all fighting over the same money for similar or overlapping initiatives. This made little sense to any of the portfolio managers and they sought the help of the business architecture team to bring clarity to the situation. Situations like this are not uncommon and require a horizontal as well as a vertical view of the enterprise from a variety of perspectives and dimensions.

Executives require better visibility into the workings of their enterprise; into relationships with customers and suppliers; into competitive impacts; and into how key decisions and projects will or will not address pressing challenges over the short and long-term. Just as the Titanic's blueprint allowed the Captain to rapidly assess the risks facing the ship and allowed him to determine the exact nature of the action to be taken, executives require a blueprint of their business. Consider the generally accepted definition of business architecture below. Business architecture is: *"A blueprint of the enterprise that provides a common understanding of the organization and is used to align strategic objectives and tactical demands."* [2]

This definition communicates the essence of business architecture – a "formal blueprint" of the business. While the Titanic's blueprint was the basis for the ship's design and construction, a business blueprint, extracted from the essence of the enterprise, serves as the foundation for business evolution and business transformation.

A Practitioner's Perspective: Man the Lifeboats or Rearrange the Deck Chairs

The purpose of a blueprint, whether of a ship, building or a city, is twofold. A blueprint provides an architectural view of a structure or a series of related structures that can be used as a basis for design and construction. The second purpose of a blueprint is to facilitate the understanding of a structure or a series of related structures in order to understand, transform or abandon that structure or structures. As a rule, we are addressing issues for organizations that already exist (versus designing new organizations). Therefore, this second use of a blueprint is applicable to a corporation, government entity, non-profit or other type of business.

Surprisingly, few organizations have a cohesive blueprint that can be used as a basis for understanding, transforming or taking other actions necessary to continue the viability of the enterprise. Not having a formal business blueprint results in poor decision making, poor deployment of good decisions and wasted resources. Consider that while the Captain of the Titanic made a rapid and correct decision to abandon ship, some of the crew continued to spend time on tasks unrelated to the emergency at hand.

Stewards continued serving drinks while other crew members worked to ensure that passengers in steerage could not enter the upper decks to try and save themselves. The crew even sent lifeboats out half empty rather than ensure the safety of as many passengers as possible. In other words, not every crew member was privy to the implications of what the Captain knew – that the ship was sinking fast and they needed to change their behavior.

In business, we face similar challenges when communicating intent and executing a cohesive strategy. We have also created political, cultural, regional and class-based roadblocks to solutions. These issues can be addressed, however, if all parties are working off of the same blueprint, but this is rarely the case. Even when executives have determined a correct course of action, redundancies and inconsistencies across business units, capabilities, processes, terminology and supporting technologies undermine solution deployments. Organizations no longer have a clear view of how the relevant parts of the enterprise fit together and this has stymied efforts to craft and deploy efficient, cost effective solutions for customer, competitive, cost and funding challenges.

Consider the situation where a multi-national business had no idea that its ship was sinking. Airbus, the European manufacturer of passenger jets that competes with Boeing, was working on a project to build the world's largest plane – the A380. The size of the plane and the project necessitated a component-based assembly approach, with each contributing country creating portions of the plane to be assembled into a single unit at a later date. Engineers from France and engineers from Germany were working on the wiring systems for the giant liner over a period of several years. Having failed to coordinate efforts to wire the world's largest plane, they were surprised to learn that they had used different approaches to designing the A380's wiring system.

German engineers employed a 2D wiring schematic while their French counterparts used a 3D wiring schematic. In order to complete the assembly of the passenger liner, the engineers were forced to extend their work to finish the plane, delaying the planned delivery date to buyers by well over a year. The result of this blunder forced a 26% drop in Airbus stock value and handed a $4.5 billion order to its chief competitor, Boeing. [3]

The Airbus situation should never have occurred and is an excellent example of an enterprise that lacked transparency into its enterprise. Ironically, the problems that arose were tied to engineers working on the blueprint of an air passenger liner, yet these same engineers and their respective business units had no blueprint of the business to guide their collaborative efforts on this massive project. Architecting and engineering buildings, planes, ships and even cities are well established professional disciplines, yet the architecting and engineering of our businesses have been left to happenstance – lacking formal blueprints for creating, understanding, navigating and transforming a business.

Consider how employing business architecture could have been used to provide transparency into the Airbus A380 initiative. The project involved organizational structures, initiatives, projects, products, assets, business capabilities, complex terminology and various business processes. A blueprint of this initiative would have provided cross-disciplinary, cross-functional transparency and allowed Airbus engineers to rapidly visualize interdependent business units that shared common business capabilities and processes, working on related projects. Under such a blueprint, collaboration emerges organically and by design – forging structural ties between business units supporting common capabilities. This is a common and proven benefit of business architecture, which in turn supports the effective deployment of good decisions and the effective deployment of critical business initiatives.

As it happened, this did not occur and the engineers continued working with the rock solid belief that they were doing the right things. In reality, these engineers were doing things right within their limited sphere of vision. The engineering teams, however, were not doing the right thing when viewed from a holistic perspective. Doing the right thing required a degree of transparency that was sorely lacking from this initiative. Airbus's ship was sinking as highly skilled professionals rearranged the proverbial deck chairs. It is not enough to have good people and good managers, because good people can do bad things when an organization has little or no insight into how all the pieces fit together.

Sorting Through the Maze of Redundant, Fragmented Business Infrastructures

Organizations, like cities, embody many seemingly disconnected and unrelated parts that are all moving in their own direction with little regard as to how the other pieces work. Everything runs smoothly until an unforeseen situation occurs such as a water pipeline break, bridge collapse or major traffic problem. The key to city planning, which uses blueprints such as the one in Figure 1.2, and the key to organizational planning both involve the ability to understand how the parts work in consort and rely on this understanding as a basis for addressing problems proactively or resolving issues quickly.

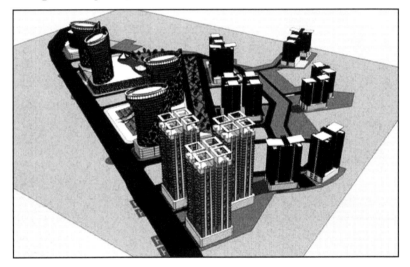

Figure 1.2: High-level City Blueprint of Kilimanjaro

The city planner, viewing the parts as they work in consort, can help minimize disruptions when they occur through various projects that preempt small problems from turning into major ones as the city grows in size and complexity. Similarly, as an organization grows in size and complexity, executives can use business architecture as a basis for taking action that preempts future problems while making the entire organization work more effectively and efficiently. In business, this typically translates into bottom line revenue growth and customer retention that collectively keeps the enterprise viable and allows it to grow and prosper.

On the flipside, inadequate city planning or a lack of attention as to how the blueprint has evolved can create problems. Some city roads seem to go in endless circles. Other cities refuse to erect overpasses or underpasses, which in turn increases traffic conjestion, introduces greater air quality issues and reduces the overall quality of life. In most circumstances, the high-level city blueprint is not enough to deploy solutions, design new structures or retrofit existing ones. Designers and engineers must be able to zoom in on key issues and this in turn requires a more detailed view of the city blueprint, as shown in Figure 2.3. Zooming in on the details facilitates detailed project planning, cost estimates and successful deployments.

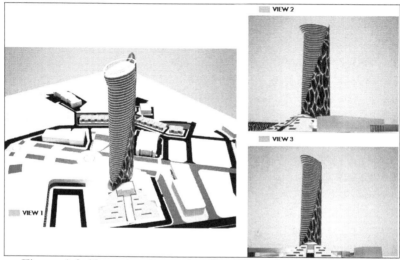

Figure 1.3: Zooming in on the City Blueprint of Kilimanjaro

In the more detailed, drill-down blueprint, shown in Figure 1.3, engineers and builders visualize the specific details required to determine a roadmap and cost out an approach for retrofitting or transforming certain structures within the context of the whole. Within a business, a project team is similarly commissioned by management to get to the details behind redundant processes, capabilities, organizational structures and other aspects of a business architecture driving up costs, driving down revenues, harming customer retention and causing a host of other problems. In organizational planning, as in city planning, high-level views trigger the need to go to the next level of detail needed to produce a solutions roadmap, project plans and cost estimates required to address these issues.

For example, proliferation of poorly aligned organizational units with split responsibilities across common business capabilities can take an organization well down the path to *dysfunction*. An example of this is having two claims units at an insurance company or two wealth management units at a bank that service an overlapping customer base. This situation could turn disastrous, as it did with the Airbus example, but could certainly be tempered if there was *transparency* to facilitate coordination and alignment across these business units.

Similarly, aligning seemingly unrelated business capabilities and responsibilities under the same executive can also take an organization down the path to dysfunction. Consider a portfolio manager at a multinational financial institution who owns the business portfolio and budgets for both the banking business and the life insurance business. While this again is not ideal, current and target views of the business architecture equip business executives with a roadmap for aligning and coordinating related business capabilities, business units, customer and supplier relationships, funding and Information Technology (IT) related resources.

From an implementation perspective, project teams may be well down the road to developing and implementing solutions to a business requirement when they discover that the solutions clash. Consider the case where business units created new interfaces for customer inquiries in parallel and did not discover that the solutions were incompatible until the business rejected these solutions for being redundant and poorly aligned. Each team rightly assumed that it did the right thing – that is, implement the *requested* business solutions. The business, however, was so disjointed that they set these teams off on parallel, conflicting paths – a dead end road as far as the city or regional blueprint is concerned.

The business blamed the implementation teams for pursuing

irreconcilable solutions, but these are not implementation team specific or IT specific issues. The real reason these situations occur is that businesses have lost their way because they lack an understanding of their current state of business and as a result have no coherent roadmap for addressing a variety of business challenges. Without a blueprint of the business, management will continue to struggle with aligning shared capabilities, processes, terminology, products, customers, suppliers and funding initiatives.

Situations like this are more commonplace than one would think and are occurring across enterprises on a scale that threatens business credibility, competitiveness, growth and overall vitality. Having a blueprint of your business can enable you to navigate a maze of dead end streets and transform the enterprise in a more cohesive, efficient and effective institution. Using the business blueprint, executives can visualize challenges, drill down to the root cause of those challenges, build consensus on the issues to be addressed, define a solution oriented roadmap that engages all constituencies and drive projects that deliver immediate business value and align with longer term strategies.

Ending the Cycle of Failed Multi-year Initiatives

As enterprises gain newfound transparency into their business, they begin to call into question big multi-year projects with seven or eight-figure price tags, elongated delivery timeframes and questionable business value. Business has routinely fallen victim to the promised nirvana of the large-scale, wipe and replace projects. This has happened because business executives have allowed IT to drive transformation agenda and have held out hope that a new set of strategic systems or software packages would fix their business problems. Clearly this has not happened.

Historically, business executives have gone along with these massive undertakings, many of which are either never delivered or dramatically scaled back after millions of dollars are spent over a multi-year window. Questionable projects are left unchecked because executives have little transparency into the business value that is or is not being achieved. This lack of transparency results in a lack of visibility into the root cause of priority issues, which in turn clouds management's ability to craft business alignment strategies needed to correct those problems. In other words, funding is being thrown at problems in the hopes that some value will be achieved.

Historically, there has been no vehicle in place for executives to know what actions should be taken by the business and by IT to enact real solutions to pressing problems. If business executives cannot visualize business issues and related solutions, then the only alternative is to let IT pursue its own solutions and blindly hope that an IT-driven solution can fix business problems. This has not worked in the past and will not work in the future.

Compounding the problems created by relying on IT driven solutions to address business issues is the concept of targeting "Holy Grail" technical architectures as solutions to business problems. One such target is called services oriented architecture or SOA. SOA has been sold heavily into the executive suite by IT and large-scale vendor partners such as IBM. We have even heard business executives parrot SOA propaganda as the solution to business problems. The latest Holy Grail solution is called "Cloud Computing," which assumes that computing services are accessible in a virtual world to address your requirements. While SOA and "the cloud" may offer some value over time, business executives must stop pouring unchecked funding and resources into technical solutions as solutions to business challenges.

Some data points help illustrate the challenges facing organizations making these large-scale investments. Studies have shown that IT has wasted billions of dollars of business's money. Standish Group research findings show that IT projects are late 72% of the time – a marked improvement over prior years. In addition, Standish Group reported that out of the $364 billion spent on IT projects for 2006, only $204 billion of this amount was considered to have delivered organizational value while $160 billion in IT spending was considered waste. [4]

These statistics refer to purchased IT solutions as well. According to Cutter Research findings, application software package solutions have fallen far short of promise. For example, 98% of business people were forced to change business processes to adjust to the new software. How many businesses feel that it is productive to completely rework virtually every business process across the enterprise? Only 28% of these projects were fully implemented; over 80% had challenges integrating these packages with in-house data; fewer than 20% of business users found it easy to achieve previously claimed benefits; and more than 60% wanted to keep the old systems. [5] The average per project price for all of this trouble was $6.4 million in the most recent year this was tracked. [6]

Business executives are beginning to wake up to these issues. One senior executive recently stated in a closed door meeting that the executive team has lost all faith in the ability of IT to drive successful implementation of projects. This statement and statements like this from other senior business executives are the beginning of the journey down the path to ending the vicious cycle of failed, multi-year projects that run into tens or hundreds of millions of dollars. This journey begins by leveraging business architecture to refocus planning, funding and investment strategies.

Business Architecture
Helps Refocus Strategic Investments

Business architecture goes beyond the notion of ensuring the success versus the failure of multi-year projects and cuts right to the heart of strategic planning and related funding. This is evidenced by the fact that executives have increasingly leaned on business architecture to help diagnose and articulate solutions to a variety of business challenges. For example, executives at one large corporation wanted to understand how existing strategies and business requirements were being supported or fulfilled through previously funded initiatives. Their question was simple. If the enterprise continues down its current path of multi-year initiatives, where will the business be in 3-5 years? One executive committee found that if the shadow of things remained unchanged, current project funding would do little to address top business priorities.

In fact, when business architecture teams provide insights into how well existing investments are being spent; management is often surprised at the findings. Major enterprises invest heavily each year into numerous initiatives with spending that runs into tens of millions of dollars on a single project and hundreds of millions of dollars annually on all projects. The Standish Group study showed that IT wastes more money annually than it actually puts to good use. So when executives want to know what they are getting for their money in relation to their top business priorities, it is no surprise that one common answer is "very little."

Consider the previous example where a senior management team determined that customer losses were mounting and that the top priority was to find out why and how current funding efforts would address these loses. The business architecture team was asked to determine why this was happening and to suggest options to address the losses. The team drafted a high-level view of customer access points, high-level processes triggered by those access points, ties via business capabilities back to applications and major data stores, and an analysis of how this environment was actually harming customers. The team then examined current initiatives that extended 3-5 years into the future to determine if any of the points of confusion would be resolved based on a collective analysis of project charters.

This approach helped executives visualize the projected impacts of these initiatives on customer losses, assuming they were all brought to successful fruition, based on a high-level snapshot of where the enterprise is at today versus a 3-5 year projection into the future. In other words, business architecture allowed management to understand the impacts of work-in-progress initiatives in relation to their top priorities. Finding that existing initiatives did little to address key executive priorities, the executive team ordered a reassessment of current projects and requested further analysis and recommendations from the business architecture team to address the customer loss requirement. The requested recommendations focused on how to meet key business objectives over the next 3-5 years.

In this example, business architecture provided the vehicle for executives to understand what was causing their customer losses, determine that their current portfolio investment strategy was inadequate to deal with these losses and establish a baseline for crafting a strategy to address these losses. In the absence of the transparency provided through the business architecture, management would have lacked insights into why they were losing customers, struggled with a fundamental understanding of existing investment impacts and been unable to come to a consensus on alternate strategies and related investment options.

Most important was the fact that the executive team could see for the first time that major funding allocations were not focused on addressing a single top priority. Executives were also armed with essential information necessary to create a revised strategy and roadmap for targeting their real requirements. In the absence of a business blueprint provided by the business architecture, executives would have continued to have an unwarranted sense of security based on the false assumption that current multi-year projects were working to address their top priorities.

One lesson in this story involves who commissioned this work. The business concerns and ultimate funding of corporate initiatives originated within the business, not within the IT organization. The initiatives found to be ineffective by the executives who commissioned this analysis were entrenched IT projects. Identifying the appropriateness of current funding efforts while concurrently addressing a critical bottom line initiative was only possible when business executives took resolute, proactive steps to do so. Wondering what the business was getting for its money was no longer good enough. Unsustainable projects needed to be stopped in their tracks.

The business must be proactive and not assume that IT is automatically going to address key business initiatives on its own. Business architecture provided essential transparency into the enterprise ecosystem required for executives to make rapid, informed decisions on critical issues undermining the business; to see how those issues were or were not being addressed based on current funding strategies; and take action to right the ship before it was too late. The good news was that there were steps that could be taken that did not involve abandoning the ship entirely – as unfortunately was not the case with the Titanic.

Stop Recreating the Wheel on Every Initiative

The head of business architecture for a large insurance company that uses consultants for a wide variety of projects stated that his business architecture provided him with a leg up on outside teams when they proposed solutions to various requirements. As a rule, when consulting companies respond to requests for proposals, the first 6-8 weeks of each project invariably involves an assessment phase geared at understanding how the various pieces fit together in the context of the problem to be solved. This pattern is repeated over and over again at organizations worldwide, typically resulting in partial snapshot of a narrow cross-section of the enterprise.

The insurance executive in the above example said he simply hands these teams the business architecture generated blueprint of the business as the baseline for beginning their project. The business blueprint gave the executive the leverage needed to ask the consulting teams to remove the 6-8 week assessment phases from each of their bids. In addition, the breadth and depth of the blueprint allowed the consultants to envision the horizontal and vertical challenges they were being asked to address and more effectively craft appropriate solutions.

Whether planning an internal project or seeking external solutions, starting over time and again with a baseline analysis of the business and IT environment leads to spiraling costs and piecemeal solutions. Most front-end assessments, regardless of the organization performing the analysis, take a narrow look at a specific issue – which is typically driven by both the business and IT. This leads to silo-based analysis, silo-based results, and ultimately to project dead-ends and failure. In a worst case scenario, upstream and downstream impacts result in unintended, highly problematic consequences for your customers.

Even when a front-end assessment is done effectively, the findings end up being packaged into a report. Critical information is buried in a myriad of disconnected, hard to build upon Word documents, diagrams and spreadsheets. Most organizations have shelves stocked full of reports and related documentation that has been collected over the years on enterprise infrastructure, business capabilities, processes and supporting systems. Unfortunately, most of this information is fragmented, redundant and lacks the cohesion needed for it to serve as the foundation for strategic planning, situation analysis and solution deployment.

As a rule, knowledge collected through these efforts remains fresh in the minds of the analysts who performed the work for the length of the project. After which point, the reports and the knowledge are typically discarded, rarely updated and almost never assimilated into a cohesive, cross-functional and cross-disciplinary blueprint. This hardly makes sense given that similar or related information is going to be collected again and again, draining scarce funding and human capital, only to be shelved or discarded.

By introducing business architecture concepts into the equation, with a focus on coalescing knowledge into a common knowledgebase and generating "on demand" blueprints of the enterprise from this knowledgebase, management can more effectively and efficiently address a wide variety of priority initiatives. Business architecture has the capability to break the cycle of reinventing the wheel on every project.

Primitive Deployments of Business Architecture

You may be thinking that you already have a business architecture established in your organization and the fact is that you
may very well have pieces of the puzzle in place. There is no
shortage of PowerPoint presentations, Visio diagrams, spreadsheets and other documents that have been used to communicate
how the business works. We have all participated in or viewed
management presentations where pictures have been used to
communicate one concept or another about a business. Add to
this the business process models that have flooded many companies and you have fragments of what one might consider business
architecture – but something is missing.

Consider that every analyst, manager and consultant tends to
bring their own variations of these pictures to the table. This information remains useful as long as the individual who created it
is there to interpret the words and pictures. In other cases more
formalized maps or models have been used to represent abstractions of the business. For example, a number of organizations use
capability maps, balanced scorecards, value streams, organization
charts and other generally accepted representations to represent
aspects of the business. Yet these views are invariably hand drawn,
disconnected from other blueprints or views, are hard to maintain
and cannot be decomposed, aggregated or analyzed beyond their
face value.

One additional challenge is that IT architecture tends to bleed
into views of the business in almost overwhelming ways. In the
recently published book, *Enterprise Architecture as Strategy,* the authors provided an interesting backdrop on business models, but
quickly dove into views of the business that were largely IT architecture based. Topics such as the "enterprise service bus," a piece
of technology that business executives have no interest in, ended
up on pictures meant to communicate the essence of the enterprise. [7]

Other works on business architecture, produced by well

meaning IT architects, include diagrams created using various modeling views from the Unified Modeling Language (UML). Business executives are not interested in looking at UML diagrams or other technical views. UML is an IT created, IT centric view of the world and has no place in the executive or management suite.

Asking some basic questions helps highlight the primitive nature of most business architecture efforts. How do all of these pieces tie together into a common view? Is there any consistency in terminology or visualization techniques? What is the foundation for this information? If something changes in the business, can it be readily reflected across all of viewpoints? Can viewpoints be connected in a way that provides a cohesive view of the business? Can viewpoints be decomposed to a level of detail necessary to support planning and implementation related activities? Can lower level views be aggregated into executive viewpoints to accommodate diverse audiences? Business architecture provides a "yes" answer to each of these questions.

The good news is that organizations are now engaging in business architecture in a way that will allow business executives and management to take charge of their destiny. This will not happen, however, if there is no solid foundation behind Power-Point and Visio diagrams. Enterprises will additionally struggle with gaining value through business architecture if IT professionals insist on delivering technical, IT centric diagrams to business professionals and executives in an effort to further their technical agendas.

Capturing the Essence of the Business in Business Architecture

Business blueprints, derived by mapping various aspects of the business into the business architecture, can represent a myriad of viewpoints spanning an enterprise and reaching into customer and supplier domains. Blueprints can also represent the enterprise at increasingly detailed levels of detail. In all cases, these blueprints or business visualizations must be based on a solid foundation or knowledgebase that represents a multidimensional mapping of abstract views of the enterprise.

One way to view what should constitute foundational aspects of business architecture is to consider what you would need to know to answer the following questions.

- What does the business do?
- Why is the business doing the things that it does?
- Who is doing these things – and to whom?
- How are things being done?

Answering these questions requires looking at specific aspects of the business, which includes any underlying concept that can be used to represent an abstract view of the business. Figure 1.4 identifies aspects of the business that form the foundation for business architecture. The categories in Figure 1.4 were derived from an industry standards group white paper [8] and also represent an industry best practices perspective on business architecture.

Figure 1.4 topic categories are abstractions of different aspects of the business and that collectively are essential to understanding, managing and transforming the business. We note that similar lists have included items such as security, but we feel that this is an abstraction that can be applied across all aspects of the categories in figure 1-4. When this information is assembled and associated with related categories, you are on your way to creating the business architecture knowledgebase.

The categories in the list are commonly understood by most business professionals. For example, a typical business establishes a vision, strategies and tactics to drive actions, projects and related activities. Other business drivers include rules, regulations and policies, which dictate how an enterprise must act within the context of an industry or government jurisdiction. A business must also interface with or respond to customers (also called constituents, patients, clients, etc.), suppliers and partners, and competitors. Customers acquire your products or services while you acquire assets and services from your suppliers and partners.

Figure 1.4: Capturing the Essence of the Business
in Business Architecture

A business can also be broken down into organizational units, such as a division, department or agency, and each unit has certain capabilities. This concept also facilitates representation of multi-enterprise business architectures. Multi-enterprise ecosystem representation may, for example, be required in situations where client or customer facing business capabilities reside within the domain of a business partner or similar entity. The concept also supports federated architecture views, which is commonly required within the U.S. Federal Government.

Business capabilities comprise what many consider the core of the business architecture because an absence of capabilities means the business does not or cannot do anything. A business capability is "a particular ability or capacity that a business may possess or exchange to achieve a specific purpose or outcome." [9] Examples of high level (or level one) capabilities include Investments, Billing, Claims or Customer Management. A business also uses terms or language to communicate internally and externally deploys business processes to accomplish a given set of tasks. Finally, a business will fund, launch and manage initiatives or projects to effect changes within and across the enterprise.

Collectively, these business categories define the essence of the business and allow us to provide answers to who does what, why they do it and how it is done. Additional questions can be addressed by building upon this foundation. For example, answering the question of how well something is being done involves putting context around this foundation. If products are to be delivered to customers within a certain timeframe of say 95% of the time, business architecture can help determine if this target is not being met. In other words, the business architecture can provide many answers to many questions, all of which are posed against an abstraction of the business contained within a business architecture knowledgebase.

These abstract views of the business, as stored within the business architecture knowledgebase, are not blueprints in and of themselves. Rather, they are the foundation from which blueprints or visual representations of the business are derived. When analyzed, abstracted and associated in various ways, business architecture provides a powerful basis for planning, developing transformational roadmaps, funding and deploying various projects, and assessing progress against strategies and plans.

Prior to introducing the business visualization concepts, it is useful to consider certain principles for organizing your business architecture knowledgebase. These principles state that business architecture:

- Represents categories of business abstractions that should be readily understood by business professionals
- Includes business categories that have naturally occurring relationships with each other and collectively provide a knowledgebase for and about the business
- Serves as a "living" source of business knowledge that evolves based on past and future discoveries from a variety of sources and projects
- Provides business professionals with only what they need to see and only when they need to see it
- Supports a zoom-in / zoom-out capability to support executives, managers and deployment teams at different levels of abstraction through the concepts of decomposition and aggregation
- Scales up and down from both horizontal and vertical perspectives
- Serves as an open environment where anyone can obtain views of the business to further the goals of the business (subject to security and confidentiality constraints)
- Can be readily mapped to IT architecture from a variety of perspectives and at varying depths of detail or breadth of coverage

We will not be getting into the mechanics of how to represent, collect and manage the business architecture knowledgebase or how to use it at this point. This will be discussed in later chapters. The main point to remember is that these concepts establish a robust foundation for business architecture that can be widely applied, to significant benefit, to satisfy a wide variety of business demands.

Visualizing the Business through Business Architecture

We distinguish between the information contained within the

business architecture knowledgebase and the many different ways in which business professionals visualize and apply this information. Abstracting aspects of a business in order to visualize those aspects in relation to a particular viewpoint or issue is similar to an architect's requirement for abstracting views of a building, ship or city.

In the latter example, various blueprints of a building or a ship can alternatively represent the electrical system, plumbing system, steel superstructure, and other viewpoints. These real world objects are represented in an abstract way to plan, design, build, refurbish or retrofit real world structures. In the case of business architecture, we are abstracting a business as opposed to a physical structure. In both cases, however, we must be able to clearly understand and articulate what it is we are abstracting and how we are representing those abstractions.

The concept of a blueprint of the business embodies many different views and can resemble what one might consider a more traditional blueprint, or take on alternative forms. For example, one such business blueprint might reflect a mapping of how customers can contact a company through a variety of entry points (e.g., email, websites, mail, agents) and trigger a highly aggregated, end-to-end business process ("value stream") which is deployed across silo-based business units through numerous redundant, low-level business processes. An example of a template for such a blueprint is shown in Figure 1.5.

One might argue that such a blueprint could be drawn up by any number of business teams or consultants, but the blueprint we are presenting here differs in several substantial ways. For one, it is a horizontal view that cuts across several lines of business and divisional structures, yet remains focused on a specific customer issue.

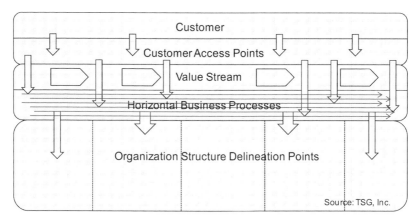

Figure 1.5: Example of a Business Blueprint Template

One issue that could be addressed using the Figure 1.5 template involves understanding why changes to customer information take so long and are performed so inconsistently. This blueprint allows business executives to understand how a customer request enters and travels across an enterprise ecosystem, where and how this occurs, and which parts of business are involved.

In addition, the connections here are not trivial or to be guessed at. One organization had scores of physical processes that had to be mapped back to a single value stream that supported a single customer related aspect of the business (i.e., updating customer contact information). This was not an academic exercise – the organization was losing customers because of the duration and fallibility of updating customer related information across different product lines and business units.

Another differentiator between the template in Figure 1.5 and historical drawings is that each abstraction of the business represented in this picture is clearly and consistently defined within the business architecture, represented in the business knowledgebase and supported by various degrees of detail that can be extracted from this knowledgebase.

When you share views such as this with executives, everyone can visualize the root cause of the issue at hand. This typically triggers a request from management to see more detail related to the exact business units involved in the customer update process as well as other information. Management may additionally request proposed options for addressing these issues. As a rule, a solution oriented roadmap requires more analysis into the business architecture as well as IT architecture engagement. Business architecture artifacts can be cross-mapped to application and data architecture artifacts to support more detailed analysis and planning efforts.

Consider a situation where planning teams have to identify the number and types of user interfaces used by each physical process as input to streamlining the customer generated update requests. Process and user interface mapping allows planning teams to associate business processes with application systems, which in turn is used to identify major data structures where customer information resides. This type of in-depth analysis of the business architecture provides the details needed to drive the creation of a strategy, execution roadmap, cost/benefit analysis and project plans to address various business challenges. Subsequent requirements may involve longer term back-end IT architecture planning to provide core IT architecture changes necessary to truly consolidate and integrate the management of customer information.

The bottom line is that if a picture is just a picture, with no supporting knowledgebase from which alternative views and more detailed assessments can be drawn, then the basis for analysis is flawed and you only have pictures – not a solid foundation for your business architecture.

Some business blueprint views may not resemble structural blueprints at all. One visualization example involves the cross-reference report where management may view how physical business processes (those actually being used by a given business team) aggregate to a logical process and ultimately to a given value stream. Other business visualization examples include familiar management tools such as the Capability Map, Porter Value

Chain, the Balanced Scorecard, Social Networking Diagram, the Supply Chain Model and many other management viewpoints that historically have never been connected to a common foundation.

This fragmentation of management viewpoints, which spawns misinformation and guesswork as to which solution is best or what problem needs to be solved, is eliminated with the advent of the business architecture knowledgebase. The knowledgebase has an unlimited potential in terms of providing transparency and clarity to the enterprise. Each analysis effort feeds and enriches the knowledgebase. As your business architecture evolves, managing, updating, cross fertilizing and producing these standardized business visualizations becomes easier because the knowledgebase expands with each assessment or project.

Mapping the Virtual Enterprise

The modern enterprise goes well beyond the legal boundaries of a given organization and extends into the realms of customers, suppliers and competitors. This is particularly true in this age of outsourcing, where business capabilities are no longer the sole domain of in-house teams. The "virtual enterprise" is a concept that recognizes that business capabilities and processes are increasingly being performed outside of the legal bounds of a given organization.

Business architecture can and should be extended into these external business domains where it is appropriate to map out aspects of the business that are not under the direct control of your organization. For example, an insurance company licensed a series of distributors to market, sell, enroll, service, bill and collect for its insurance products. All client facing business capabilities were outsourced to these third parties while all non-client facing capabilities such as actuarial, reinsurance, investment and product management remained in-house.

The virtual insurance ecosystem was quite complex when viewed as a whole. There was a lack of clarity as to who was responsible for a given capability and certain business processes were co-opted by various parties. There were two major considerations in this example. The first involved ensuring that the organization and its partners worked to stay competitive in the face of growing and fierce competition from larger, monolithic companies. The second consideration involved the allocation of funding and resources across the virtual ecosystem.

Prior to mapping the business architecture for this virtual enterprise, it was difficult to determine the root cause and response to a variety of issues. Once the ecosystem was mapped into the business architecture, however, it brought clarity to roles and responsibilities for business professionals across the virtual enterprise. The business architecture provided a blueprint of the virtual enterprise; and included organization unit and business capability mapping, which drove new ways of thinking, allowed teams to focus on cross-organizational alignment and opened up communication paths that were previously unknown or poorly defined.

As client facing capabilities became a focal point, collaborative teams were assembled with representatives from each company to address ongoing issues, streamline business processes and, where necessary, serve as a focal point for driving business and IT alignment. As this occurred, the insurance company could focus more of its efforts on streamlining non-client facing capabilities, processes, roles and responsibilities to improve overall business performance, compliance and profitability.

We must note at this point that the practice of business architecture is meant to be as pragmatic as possible. For example, the entire business knowledgebase is rarely created or populated all at once, but rather, is expanded upon when driven by a specific management request or when management feels that it is appropriate to expand the business architecture knowledgebase for one reason or another.

Establishing your business architecture, and optionally ·expanding it to represent the virtual enterprise, opens up an entire world of possibilities in terms of the kinds of information that executives, managers, planning teams and implementation teams can access and leverage. The world of business architecture offers significant possibilities for business to drive strategy through execution and turn back the tide of being a passive bystander as consultants and IT drive their own visions forward.

Business Architecture, IT Architecture and Enterprise Architecture

We defined business architecture at the beginning of this chapter but we should clarify a couple of other terms that are in common use today. Interestingly, as of the time of this writing, the terms IT architecture and enterprise architecture have no common industry definitions. Therefore, we feel it important that we clarify our use of these terms as they arise in later chapters of this book.

Given that we introduced the industry standard definition of business architecture as being a "blueprint of the business," we will use the term "IT architecture" to mean a blueprint of the information technology that supports the business. IT architecture has three commonly agreed upon areas of focus: application architecture, data architecture and the technical architecture. We will get into more detail on IT architecture and its role in business transformation and alignment in chapter four. For now it is only important to keep in mind that IT architecture refers to blueprints of IT application systems, data and technology while business architecture refers to blueprints of the business itself – which includes the IT organization as a business unit.

A second definition, which invariably comes to mind when discussing business architecture and IT architecture, involves the concept of "enterprise architecture." For our purposes, enterprise architecture is the combined view of the business architecture and IT architecture. Historically, the term enterprise architecture has a tendency to turn off business professionals because they immediately assume that the concept is an IT focused creation. For this reason, we will stay clear of the term enterprise architecture in subsequent chapters and always strike a clear line of delineation between business architecture and IT architecture.

Regarding business and IT alignment, we discuss business and IT mapping and alignment in Chapter 4, focusing on the "touch points" between the business architecture and IT architecture. Moving forward it is important to remember two key points. IT architecture is aligned to or in conjunction with business architecture but business architecture must also recognize advances in technology that provide business value. IT architecture, however, is never meant to dictate how a business should be run.

Ultimately the business must determine where it wants to go, how quickly it wants to get there and how to fund such efforts. This business alignment approach may involve consolidating or aligning business units, business capabilities, business processes and business semantics to achieve a specific set of business objectives. When business driven alignment is sidestepped and IT attempts to drive consolidation, process automation or other business centric initiatives, the business can grow even more poorly aligned. Conversely, a synchronized approach to business and IT alignment ensures that IT evolves with the business and the business evolves with IT.

Current State vs. Future State Business Architecture

Another important point involves understanding the current state view of business architecture and IT architecture where appropriate. Current state and future state analysis is critical to understanding and communicating the required steps that must go into addressing critical business requirements. Current state analysis is typically sidestepped in favor of jumping to a solution without understanding the breadth and depth of the problem.

When the current state business architecture is not understood, then you have no foundation for your business architecture. Even more problematic is the common misunderstanding of whether someone is discussing the current state or the target state of the business (or IT) architecture. We have even seen presentations where an architect called the picture a "current state plus one" view of the business and IT architecture. The plus one view assumed that all projects currently underway would be completed successfully, on time and on budget, one year from today. This is a target state view, not a current state view.

We will cover the role of current state and future state mapping, and the role this plays in strategic planning in later chapters. For now, keep in mind that the current state and the future state play equally important roles in communicating and addressing critical business issues. Watts Humphrey once said that "if you don't know where you are, a map won't help."[10] As such, the current state is an essential aspect of any business architecture effort and creates the baseline for assessment movement to the target state of the business.

A Framework for Business Architecture

There are several aspects to business architecture that we have introduced to this point including the business architecture knowledgebase and visualization capabilities that provide the foundation for situation analysis and resolution. When coupled with the concept of business architecture scenarios, it establishes a framework for business architecture deployment. Figure 1.6 depicts the business architecture framework.

The framework in Figure 1.6 shows how business architecture scenarios, which are project oriented templates that facilitate the assessment and resolution of a wide variety of business challenges, leverage the business architecture knowledgebase. Scenarios determine which aspects of the business should be visualized, drive target state architecture requirements and establish business transformation requirements that spawn subsequent deployment projects.

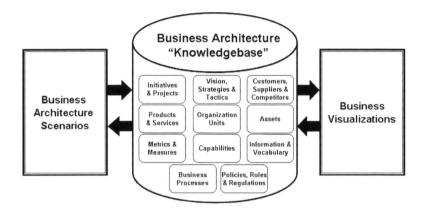

Figure 1.6: Business Architecture Framework

Scenarios will be considered in more depth in Chapter 5 when we discuss business architecture in practice.

We will revisit the framework concept as our discussion proceeds. The key aspect to remember is that for business architecture to deliver sustainable value to an enterprise requires the knowledgebase, visualization capabilities and scenarios to guide management planning and deployment options.

What's Next?

We discussed why business architecture matters to business professionals by providing user stories citing how business architecture benefits an organization as well as the downsides of ignoring business architecture. We also provided the foundational underpinnings for business architecture, introduced the business architecture knowledgebase concept and discussed how business architecture supports visualizing the enterprise from many perspectives, including the understanding of the virtual enterprise. In addition, we discussed the role of business architecture within the context of IT architecture and business and IT alignment.

In the following chapters we will provide you with details as to how to establish your business architecture knowledgebase, create visualizations and blueprints of your business, setup your business architecture team, aligning IT architecture with your business and getting started. In addition to interjecting more user stories, we will be discussing how various business scenarios play out when the benefits of business architecture are brought into the picture.

Business architecture is here to stay. The organizations that take advantage of business architecture will see considerable value to themselves and their customers. This will allow business to take ownership of the strategic agenda, define the roadmaps and related funding necessary to achieve that agenda and gain more value for their project investments.

References

[1] "Aligning Technology and Business: Applying Patterns for Legacy Transformation," Howard Hess, IBM Systems Journal, Volume 44 Number 1, 2005, http://www.research.ibm.com/journal/sj/441/hess.pdf

[2] Business Architecture Working Group, http://bawg.omg.org

[3] "In Tangles of Airbus Project, a Reflection of Europe's Struggles," John Ward Anderson, Washington Post Foreign Service, April 27, 2007

[4] "Chaos Summary 2008: The 10 Laws of Chaos," Standish Group, 2008

[5] "Application Package Software: The Promise vs. Reality," Appendix E, Vol. 6, No. 9 Cutter Benchmark Review, William Ulrich, 2006

[6] "The Cost of ERP," 2002, http://www.standishgroup.com/chaos/beacon_243.php

[7] "Enterprise Architecture as Strategy," HBS Press, Jeanne W. Ross, Peter Weill, David C. Robertson, 2009

[8] "Defining Requirements for a Business Architecture Standard," McWhorter & Ulrich, 2009, htp://bawg.omg.org/Bus_Arch_Ecosystem_White_Paper_Draft.pdf

[9] "A Business-Oriented Foundation for Service Orientation," Ulrich Homann, Feb. 2006, http://msdn.microsoft.com/en-us/library/aa479368.aspx

[10] "Managing the Software Process," Watts Humphrey, SEI, 1989

Two

The Transparent Enterprise

What is needed is a relativistic theory, to give up altogether the notion that the world is constituted of basic objects or building blocks. Rather one has to view the world in terms of the universal flux of events and processes.
—David Bohm

Executives today have more visibility into the internal working of their organization than at any point in history. Technology has made it possible for individuals to gain real-time access to the operations in their organizations at a level that could only be imagined just a few short years ago. But in spite of this vast new pool of information, executives find that they struggle still to gain real insight into what is going on in their organization. Executives are now faced with the dilemma of information overload. With so much information available how is it that someone can navigate to what is important?

Executives are looking for tools that can help bring order to this chaos. We bring order by creating abstractions that simplify a problem and bring focus to the key aspects of a situation. In fact if we did capture every little detail the picture would be so complex that it would be almost impossible to understand. In the building architecture community they use blueprints as a way of creating this kind of abstraction. A blueprint typically does not provide the exact details of how a structure is built. What makes the blueprint valuable is that it provides a way to quickly understand the major structural elements of a project and how they interrelate. In short, the blueprint provides a level of transparency to how a structure is organized that allows individuals to more rapidly assess the impact of any attempt to modify the structure.

The Need for Visibility

Organizations might be best thought of as a hive of individuals all generally working toward a common goal. In this hive or social network, most participants do not have much visibility into how their work contributes to the big picture of the hive's overall well being. Individuals go about their days making the decisions that are needed to deal with the expected and unexpected situations that they encounter based upon the context that they work within. This kind of organizational structure functions pretty well in most situations, however there are kinds of situations where this kind of approach fails with what can be serious consequences.

One of these situations is what we might think of as being the "extrapolating one step too far" fallacy. This problem has been well understood in engineering for some time. It involves taking an existing practice and applying it to a new situation without critically reevaluating whether or not the tradeoffs that were made in the original situation still hold in the new one. It is not too hard to see how this happens when an organization is in a hurry to expand into a new market or introduce a new product line. One Canadian steel fabricator relates his experience with creating a new unit to expand into the U.S. market:

We learned we did not understand the USA market and that it functioned very differently to that in Canada. Many market-related assumptions were in error... It was closed in 1988. [1]

Another situation is not as widely recognized but is equally serious. In this case an organizationally significant decision is made without recognition that this is actually happening. It is not hard to see how these kinds of things happen either. Organizations often see a major opportunity to address an issue in one area without pausing to fully understand the implications to the broader organization. The use of outsourcing has been a case in point for many organizations. An alliance manager for telecommunications infrastructure and network for Chevron, observed this about the business process outsourcing trend:

"Unfortunately, a lot of companies made some mistakes, because they didn't realize all of the implications associated with outsourcing, and they didn't have the internal structures to manage it effectively," he states. "As a result, many of them failed." [2]

When just one of these two situations occurs, the consequences can be considerable. But when both situations occur the consequences can be much more serious. When an organization both extrapolates too far and then fails to understand that there are significant implications to the broader organization, then they are flirting with disaster.

When Visibility Breaks Down:
The Hyatt Regency Crown Center Disaster

This confluence of both of these forces is most dramatically visible in an industry where what is being produced is tangible. The construction engineering industry is one of the most mature industries in terms of structured and accountable practices. Likely this reflects the profound implications associated with a major structural failure. When things go wrong they are often calamitous. Because of this, incidents are also thoroughly investigated to understand what allowed the failure to happen.

On July 17, 1981 the Hyatt Regency Crown Center hotel in Kansas City, Missouri suffered a calamitous event. On that day a set of suspended passageways collapsed killing 114 people and injuring more than 200 others. [3] The investigation that followed this tragedy revealed that the collapse was the result of a combination of several different factors.

The first step in this disaster was a design change that was made by the contractor. The original design called for a set of long support rods to be attached to beams above the passageways. The rods would pass thru and attach to each of the three passageways. This design entailed a complex and problematic assembly process so the contractor requested a change so that the rods could be shorter. Instead of a set of continuous rods the new shorter rods would connect first to the highest passageway and then a new set of rods would connect from that passageway to the next lower one and similarly for the next passageway. As the overall weight and structure of the passageways was not changing, the design change did not seem significant.

However, the new design meant that the top-most passageway was now carrying the weight of the two lower passageways instead of this weight being carried by the beams above the passageways as the original design had lain out. By modifying the design, the contractor had simply implemented a well-known design alternative. Unfortunately, the new design pattern, shown in Figure 2.1, extended beyond the design capacity of the passageways.

Figure 2-1: View of the 4th floor support beam,
during the first day of the investigation of the
Hyatt Regency walkway collapse [4]

These kinds of changes are commonplace in the building engineering trades, so there are typically procedures in place that call for the review and evaluation of the impact of these kinds of changes. If procedures existed to examine exactly these kinds of changes how could it be that this problem was not found? Miscommunication between the architects and the subcontractors was fundamental to the catastrophe. As a result of this miscommunication the architectural firm did not realize that a significant design change had taken place and no reassessment of the design proposed by the contractor was performed. The lack of visibility into the changes and the impacts of those changes created an opening that allowed a standard design technique to be applied with disastrous consequences.

Existing Levels of Transparency Are Not Enough

Thankfully the direct consequences to human life are usually much fewer for most organizations than they are for building architects and engineers. The impact of an organization's failure to realize when it is misaligned typically runs from wasted investment to missing out on a major new market or market shift. However, the indirect human impact of these kinds of mistakes can be enormous since these mistakes can lead major organizations or even industries into decline based on how well they navigate these challenges.

With all of the investment in management systems it might seem that a modern organization would have all the information that they could possibly need. And in some ways this is certainly the case. Organizations have invested in ERP systems to provide detailed operational data in something close to real-time. And to make sense of all that information many organizations have created comprehensive corporate dashboards to provide visualizations and roll-ups of the information embedded in those systems. Those systems have helped provide organizations with transparent knowledge of all their operations. ERP have done this by helping organizations keep inventory levels low, providing forecasting capabilities for purchasing and by supporting manufacturing and distribution decisions.

These systems are primarily focused on monitoring the operation and monitoring how those operations are performing against benchmarks. Within organizations that are awash with all this data it is still common to hear people bemoan the fact that these systems fail to accurately deliver a measure of the total value of various enterprise investments. The reason is that these systems focus on quantifiable measures of return. While this is an important aspect of any organization, the focus on purely quantifiable measures leaves out any assessment of the value associated with investments that have not been fully realized.

Value-focused investment analysis is excluded simply because it is difficult to fit it into a quantifiable economic model. The kinds of things that end up being excluded include: supporting new business opportunities, increasing speed to market, retaining customers and increasing the productivity of innovation. These kinds of benefits are sometimes referred to as capabilities. We can think of these as benefits that have been enabled and have the potential to create directly measurable operational benefits, but which have not yet been used to provide those benefits. This is an important distinction because most organizations have multiple significant investments underway at any point in time. Many of these investments require the coordination of efforts across the entire organization over some extended period of time. It is during this period of time that traditional operational monitoring techniques do not provide much support.

We can think of this distinction as being between a retrospective point of view and a prospective point of view as illustrated in Figure 2.2.

Figure 2.2: Seeing what has been or seeing what will come to be

Retrospective viewpoints include information on things like financial measures, process metrics, market share, customer surveys and so on. In order for these business views to be meaningful, we need to establish a much broader enterprise perspective that incorporates planned or in progress initiatives and the impact these initiatives have on customers, products, capabilities, information, processes and related IT assets. Unfortunately, too much work is going on that is hidden from the very business professionals that need to understand the impacts of that work the most.

Because there is not any retrospective data to measure until the work being done comes to fruition the result is that these activities remain hidden. Unfortunately, what you *cannot* see *can* hurt you. Sadly, this situation is all too common for the vast majority of enterprises. Organizations find themselves managing in the rear view mirror through a retrospective view of their business. Organizations are painfully aware of the dangers of these kinds of efforts. These new efforts are difficult to successfully benchmark and cost equations are difficult to create.

The reason behind this difficulty is that the full implications are difficult to map out in advance for innovation intensive efforts such as these. As a result, organizations often fall back onto the *"numbers don't lie"* approach and insist on trying to quantify the benefits. The hard numbers game is further magnified by the fact that most organizations have taken to heart a phrase that has become a rallying cry for a generation of MBAs, "you can't manage what you can't measure." But what are the implications of failing to find a way to deal with these kinds of initiatives?

While the traditional operational metrics approach is essential to creating bottom-line profitability, this line of thinking makes it hard for organizations to support investment in new capabilities that require a series of coordinated efforts to develop. In a competitive marketplace these new capabilities are what position an organization to be able to differentiate itself in the market. We can see this tension playing out in organizations at the program and project levels as well as at the portfolio management and executive level. Managers find that they are pulled between two opposite demands: to deliver value with every project and to move the organization along to address long-standing problems that stand in the way of key strategic goals. In fact many organizations refuse to fund any initiative that cannot, on its own, show that it can reach whatever threshold ROI measure is set by that organization's executive committee.

But what if the value of the delivery of some set of initiatives is greater than the sum of the benefits directly attributable to each of the projects? The answer is often that an individual leading an initiative has to find a way to accomplish both objectives while still meeting the organization's project-based benefits measures. Given the difficulty that organizations have in tracking how multi-project, multi-year initiatives fit together and whether they are really delivering the benefits that were promised, most have opted to simply say no.

What would it take for an organization to get beyond this kind of paralysis? While there is no single answer there is one answer that rises above the others and that answer is...*transparency*. Instead of simply saying that you can't manage what you can't measure, we need to say that you can't manage what you can't visualize. For projects that are enabling new capabilities or even modifying existing capabilities, traditional operational metrics do not provide the kind of visibility that is needed. This requires a prospective view of your enterprise – a view that is achieved through the transparency brought by business architecture.

A Different Kind of Transparency

Virtually all organizations have the ability to see a snapshot, at some level, of how their organization is faring. That ability allows them to keep an eye on how well the organization is meeting its objectives on a daily or sometimes even a real-time basis. This information is often presented in the form of a *dashboard* that consolidates data into a format that makes it easier to quickly grasp the key performance characteristics. These characteristics typically cover the organization's financial data at the very least and often extend into monitoring of operational outputs and related metrics.

These dashboards allow an organization to drill down through various financial and operational metrics to decompose these measures into their constituent components. So an executive can drill down on a division that is not meeting targeted profitability ratio and determine whether the issue is sales driven or cost driven. On the sales side they might drill down to see if a sales driven issue is driven by specific product lines, specific geographic areas or other market conditions while on the cost side they might drill down to see if labor or raw materials were the major contributors and then drill down to see what particular material or what particular set of facilities were responsible for the issues.

This kind of drill-down works well because the information being drilled into has two key characteristics: it is readily quantifiable and it is computationally decomposable. The information is considered readily quantifiable because there are metrics within the operation of the organization that can be directly measured to find the values we need. Quantifiably decomposable refers to the ability of lower level metrics to be algorithmically combined to compute the higher level metric as shown in the example in Figure 2.3. These are characteristics typical of retrospective data collected from operational elements of an organization.

$$ROE = \frac{Net\ Income}{Sales} * \frac{Sales}{Total\ Assets} * \frac{Total\ Assets}{Stockholders\ Equity}$$

Figure 2.3: Drilling down on Return on Equity
using the standard "DuPont" Decomposition [5]

Yet despite all the information these dashboards contain, they provide only a very limited view into an organization. This kind of information is focused on capturing how an organization *has* performed so when organizations turn to innovation processes these dashboards are more like empty slates. Innovation initiatives typically have a significant period during the investment portion of an initiative's lifecycle where they are not expected to make any operational contribution. Because of this, there is not any retrospective data to present.

Baseline data is a common approach used to figure out how well a particular initiative is progressing. But because innovation implies a level of uncertainty, measures of progress are themselves hard to define with confidence, making base-lining difficult. Organizations often confront questions like:

- *Exactly how much effort will it take to expand into another market?*
- *How much investment will be required to produce the next generation of a product?*
- *When will the upgraded customer support system be able to fully replace the existing systems performing this role?*

Getting visibility into how well a business is aligning to its objectives is a significant departure that goes beyond the numerically based operational measures management uses today. What is required is a different approach to transparency. This approach involves tying together a myriad of supporting decisions that are not easily quantified and often were not even known when the initiative's objectives were established. What we need is a way of monitoring the decisions and rationales associated with strategic objectives that allows us to drill down through organizational layers, visualize the decisions, initiatives and related impacts of implementing those objectives, and tie high-level objectives to lower level objectives.

When we talk about being able to trace how an organization goes about achieving its objectives through various activities within that organization, we are treading on the home turf of business architecture. The primary role of an organization's business architecture is to support exactly this kind of visibility in order to allow an organization to gain alignment across different areas within the organization. Business architecture supports this by tying together an organization's objectives, the work that an organization is performing and the rationales that link these. By building an integrated business architecture knowledgebase we gain the ability to look inside the activities of an organization and have visibility into the series of decisions that are being made daily to evaluate their contribution to organizational objectives.

Applying a business architecture-based approach to this problem allows organizations to visualize "who," "what," "where," "why" and "how" initiatives evolve from both a holistic and a detailed perspective. The knowledgebase provides a way to gain greater visibility into organizational objectives, the rationales supporting these objectives and the prospective impacts of implementing them. In turn, this greater degree of transparency provides valuable information to support more creativity at lower levels while instilling a governance capability that was not possible using the traditional dashboard approach.

Traditional operational metrics are an essential piece of the organizational dashboard, but in these increasingly complex times, these metrics are just not enough. The robust business architecture is essential to moving forward with a more sophisticated approach that facilitates and motivates the organizational innovation that firms need to differentiate themselves in today's environment.

The Business Architecture Dashboard

If a traditional executive dashboard does not provide what is needed to support innovation initiatives then we need something else. That something else is a "business architecture dashboard." This dashboard represents an integrated approach to business architecture visualization as introduced in Chapter 1. Unlike traditional dashboards, such as the one depicted in Figure 2.4, a business architecture dashboard is a way of seeing into work that has yet to deliver its operational benefit. To understand how such a dashboard can help provide this kind of insight we need to examine the kind of process that most organizations follow today.

The metrics and viewpoints reflected in the sample dashboard in Figure 2.4 reflect retrospective metrics. While these are useful to the sales unit and enterprise executives on the whole, the dashboard metrics and viewpoints do not provide transparency into weaknesses in the business blueprint such as process redundancy, failure to align with strategic market outreach initiatives, and related views that show what work is underway to address these issues.

Most major organizations have a series of complex projects

underway that contain interrelated dependencies. Often times those projects have both tactical goals that have concrete and specific operational benefits as well as strategic goals that contribute to overall improvement in the organization's capabilities. To deal with this diverse set of objectives, management oftentimes creates a gated strategic approval process for controlling the progress of a major initiative as it moves through key stages of the process.

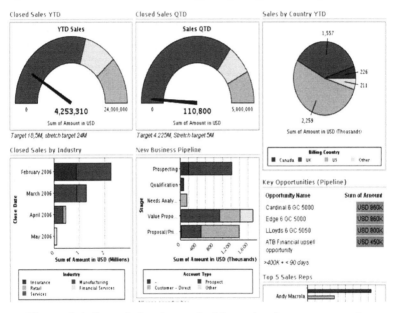

Figure 2.4: Sample business dashboard using retrospective metrics (Source: http://adminexchange.wordpress.com/)

For example, executives may insist that a market evaluation be completed, as well as a skills evaluation and an analysis of the investment costs and determination of related projected benefits. But most innovation initiatives involve benefits that require coordination across multiple business units and related initiatives. Monitoring the way in which these related projects support the achievement of higher level objectives is difficult. And because initiatives evolve and morph as they move forward, existing project governance approaches do not provide the visibility into the evolving relationships among these initiatives.

This lack of holistic project and program synchronization can be strategically debilitating. To illustrate the point let us take a quick look at the issues faced by one organization. A major insurance company had multiple strategic programs that it was pursuing. As part of their gated process they evaluated each of the programs to determine how they were aligned with and contributing toward improving the major business objectives that had been set by the executive leadership committee.

One of those business objectives was to consolidate the multiple views of the customer that had grown up within the organization via acquisitions and through the evolution of different business lines into a single "one customer" integrated viewpoint. Each program was vetted for its contribution to this "one customer" objective. Yet several years into the execution of these programs, the company found that only the most minimal movement toward the "one customer" objective had been made.

What happened to this organization is surprisingly commonplace. First, as the programs moved ahead, the focus became more and more upon the concrete deliverables that were established by the various projects chartered within the programs. Because it did not make sense to initiate "one customer" projects directly, this work was piggy-backed on other projects within each of the programs. The individual projects were held accountable for the concrete outcomes that they could achieve and as the pressure to make tradeoffs mounted, extraneous capabilities aimed at delivering a piece of the grand "one customer" objective were sacrificed.

While it might be tempting to see this as a failure to hold the programs accountable for their contribution to the "one customer" objective, it is probably more accurate to see this as a failure to visualize the end-state business architecture from a holistic perspective. The lack of a clear definition of what the "one-customer" end-state capabilities, semantics and processes would look like made it likely that even if the individual projects had attempted to deliver their piece of the puzzle, the end results would not have been a cohesive solution to the one-customer business problem. In other words, all of the pieces were unlikely to coalesce into a strategic solution even if each project did not devolve into its own silo-based solution.

In order for an organization to monitor its alignment to strategic, cross-functional objectives, a project governance structure that leverages the business architecture framework needs to be established to track how those objectives are being achieved at each stage of the current-to-target business architecture alignment process. The end goal is not to develop a single comprehensive model of the enterprise. Rather, the idea is to exercise the business architecture framework in a way that links strategic and the operational initiatives to the ongoing activities that are being performed across organizational units and subunits.

The ultimate structure of such a knowledgebase and the overall framework must be driven by the particular makeup and requirements of a given organization, although best practices provide an excellent starting point. The idea behind the framework is to create a scalable, flexible capability for an organization to be able to link how multiple parallel, scenario-driven initiatives simultaneously support both strategic and operational improvements that leverage the business architecture dashboard.

Behind the Dashboard:
The Business Artifact Knowledgebase

In order to support this kind of business architecture dashboard, it is essential for an organization to go beyond retrospective metrics. To actually build a functioning dashboard requires creating the business architecture knowledgebase. This knowledgebase contains information about the various business elements and the relationships among these business elements defined within the business architecture knowledgebase. In order to bring such a knowledgebase into existence, organizations would need to create a repository as the source of this business information, which would allow various business professionals to extract information about ongoing initiatives and get answers about where things stand and how projects impact the business.

The best way to understand the knowledgebase concept is by taking a look at how this would work in practice. Let us go back to the example we were talking about before with the organization that wanted to move toward a "one customer" objective. The executive committee had identified this "one customer" objective as one of the key goals for the organization to pursue. Along with this objective the organization had identified several benefits: improved customer loyalty, increased cross-selling and reduced and more focused communication to customers. Attached to these benefits were various metrics such as: reduced customer turnover, improved customer satisfaction rating and increased product per customer ratio.

Having established the objectives and metrics for assessing whether the benefits were achieved, management could then dispatch the strategic initiatives committee to vet all programs and major capital projects against these and assess their progress with achieving them. It was at this point that this organization, like many other organizations, ran into trouble. Because they had no clear approach for translating their strategic planning processes into an ongoing governance structure, management had only limited visibility into their work in progress.

As the organization moved forward, different areas developed key deliverables that they believed would support the strategic objectives. These deliverables reflected each area's best judgment about where to invest in creating new capabilities as well as investment in specific process improvement areas. However, because these individual approaches were not integrated through using business architecture, the way that each of these initiatives supported these goals and their strategic impacts were difficult to evaluate. This in turn resulted in executives that were unwilling to commit to funding resources that these projects required. What made it so difficult for this organization to see how their investment would be realized?

Process change and innovation involves a combination of business and IT change. Many organizations have structured themselves so that they are organizationally aligned by processes and, therefore, can track costs to processes. The same generally cannot be said, however, about IT costs. Most IT costs are tracked as overhead assigned to whatever level of organization that particular IT area is accountable to. So when an initiative is undertaken within IT to support a business change effort, the traceability generally begins and ends as an allocation back to one or more business areas. Gaining greater transparency into the relationship between IT costs and business initiatives is a key scenario that illustrates the need for an overall business architecture, related knowledgebase, framework for managing this information and a dashboard for tracking it.

Pursuing Business Aims: Applying the Knowledgebase

Using the business architecture knowledgebase would facilitate analysis of this situation. Figure 2.5 depicts a relationship structure within the knowledgebase that maps relevant artifacts necessary to track multiple projects that impact a common set of business information, business capabilities and business processes. The artifacts and relationships shown in Figure 2.5 capture the concepts introduced in Chapter 1 and reflect a typical view of these relationships.

Using the structure shown in Figure 2.5 an organization can go beyond what we have discussed in the example. This business architecture knowledgebase also makes it possible to track initiatives to the organization unit that is pursuing the initiative. In addition, this structure makes it possible to tie together the funded programs and projects that have been chartered to pursue those initiatives. The relationships within the business architecture knowledgebase provide management with the information it needs to visualize in order to bring improved transparency to large-scale, multi-year funding of a customer consolidation effort. Note that while the structure of the knowledgebase is based upon a standard schema the exact configuration use will also be shaped by a particular organization's requirements for the business architecture knowledgebase visualization.

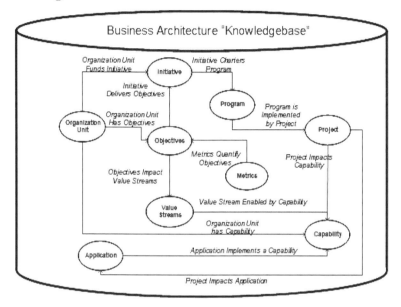

Figure 2.5: Sample view of business artifact relationships within the knowledgebase

This structure facilitates a broad based analysis of the customer related business capabilities, value streams, process and information across the silos of the enterprise, how each business unit relies on or utilizes the information and processes, and which planned or in-progress projects will or are impacting each of these areas. Using this structure also makes it possible for metrics to be developed that identify the scope of complexity involved in the customer consolidation effort that we examined earlier.

While this structure provides executives with a tool to assess the progress and impacts of the work being done the business architecture knowledgebase has additional benefits. This structure can also be used to ensure that all parties are aware of how other workers in the "hive" are impacting, contributing to or slowing down the overall effort to achieve customer consolidation. Consider some of the following metrics that can be derived from the repository view in Figure 2.5.

- Business units requiring consolidation
- Number of physical business processes tied to customer information updating
- Number of concurrent projects focused on customer related business capabilities
- Number of planned projects focused on customer related process and information consolidation

Having these metrics offers the management team a way to visualize the situation by providing a prospective view as to how to correct course on multiple, related projects running in parallel across disparate business units. Based on this information, let us take another look at the concept of a prospective dashboard, shown in Figure 2.6.

Figure 2.6 depicts several viewpoints of the business that look at the cross-functional impacts of customer consolidation along with a future projection that consolidation will be achieved in a 5-year window. These sample viewpoints are forward looking and based on information within the business architecture knowledgebase. Other views may be produced depending on the initiatives planned or underway, the level of information desired or required by a given audience, and the needs of a particular area of the enterprise at a given point in time.

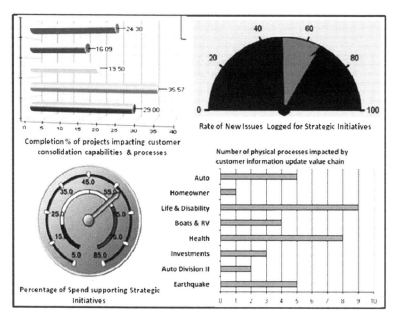

Figure 2.6: Sample "business architecture dashboard"
based on prospective metrics

Exercising the Business Architecture Dashboard

By integrating a business architecture framework into an organization it becomes possible to create a governance structure that provides a new and powerful level of transparency to the enterprise. While the exact makeup and structure of the business architecture framework and underlying knowledgebase depends upon the nature of a particular organization, best practices provide a template for moving forward. For example, in the customer consolidation scenario discussed earlier in this chapter, we recommended certain relationships within the knowledgebase that, once established, would provide a much greater degree of transparency to the overall governance structure of the initiatives aimed at achieving consolidation.

If we look back at our example we can identify several governance approaches that might have provided significant value to the organization in its pursuit of the "one customer initiative. First, the organization could have established a high-level conceptual set of processes as end-state targets for how a "one-customer" approach would have worked. We introduced this in chapter one as the value stream concept. This highly aggregated process definition should be considered a general roadmap that would need to evolve as the strategic objective moves closer and closer to fruition. And to make sure that this does not get lost in the shuffle, assigning a steward to this end-to-end process transformation is essential. Next, existing processes need to be evaluated to determine if they can be changed to support the needs or if there are structural limitations that need to be addressed to enable the change.

The idea of structural limitations is one that most organizations have probably encountered. Structural limitations are situations where an organization identifies candidate "capabilities" that are prerequisites for an initiative. Developing these capabilities requires investments that frequently have benefits outside of the particular project that identifies the capabilities. Within each project it is possible to identify the processes and activities that require these capabilities and to identify how each of these impacts a particular benefit and the metrics that can be expected to be impacted by those changes. Any new capabilities that projects are delivering would need to be reconciled with the set of strategic capability investments previously identified or escalated to the process steward so that they can consider developing a modified process definition and presenting it for reevaluation as part of any strategic planning process.

While many organizations in principle follow something similar to the approach outlined, in practice the adherence to it is generally poor. The issue that drives organizations away from this kind of approach is the lack of a knowledgebase to allow integrated on-demand visibility into this information. In practice that means that this information is gathered and reevaluated infrequently. That, in turn, means that organizations have trouble making progress on efforts such as the one that we have been discussing. It also means that misalignment occurs frequently and is not caught until relatively late creating sometimes significant costs, both in time and in money, to deal with the associated rework.

Beyond the Dashboard: Common Business Architecture Visualizations

In Chapter 1, we showed an example of a knowledgebase-derived, executive level visualization that represented a customer information update scenario under review by the executive team. It is important to recognize that there are a number of other visual representations management can leverage to increase enterprise transparency. Each of these visualizations represents a different way of viewing the contents of the business architecture knowledgebase. One commonly used representation is the "capability map." We discussed business capabilities as defining "what" a business can do. Capabilities define the range of behaviors that an organization has available to deliver business benefits. Figure 2.7 provides an example of a level one capability map.

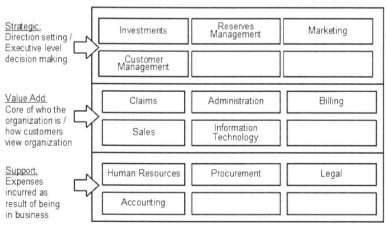

Figure 2.7: Partial, level one Capability Map

Level one business capabilities, which can be shown on a single page as in Figure 2.7, represent the highest level view of what a business does. Capabilities are frequently broken down into finer levels of granularity using a hierarchical structure. Level two and level three decompositions provide more detail and the map would be expanded accordingly. For example, the "Procurement" capability decomposes into level two capabilities "Manage Vendors" and "Manage Product Acquisition." Similarly, the level two capability "Manage Vendors" decomposes into level three capabilities that include "Manage Vendor Information" and Manage Vendor Contracts."

Figure 2.7 also represents the common value analysis convention of categorizing capabilities by strategic, value add and supporting categories which allows executives to focus their attention on the top two categories while potentially outsourcing the value add category. This is an example of a customization of the business architecture framework. These categorizations can change depending on organizational priorities and industry related factors. Procurement, for example, would likely fall into the strategic category for a manufacturing firm such as Toyota. Finally, executives use a variation of the capability map called a "heat map." A heat map is a capability map that has color coded capabilities based on measures of importance and related challenges associated with that capability. For example, red is used to indicate that the executive team should focus on that capability because it is on the critical path for multiple initiatives.

By coupling capabilities with organizational views using the business architecture knowledgebase, you can visualize "who" is doing "what." Figure 2.8 is a social network diagram that has been adopted for business architecture and draws directly on the information mappings within the business architecture knowledgebase. In Figure 2.8, you can see how the enterprise has a number of top level business units, such as "Property and Casualty" that have certain capabilities, such as "Billing" or "Claims."

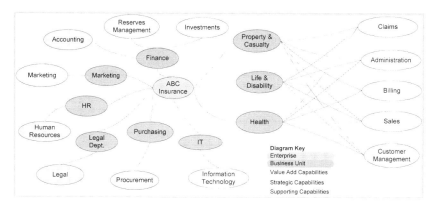

Figure 2.8: Business unit, capability level one
social networking diagram & redundancy mapping

Figure 2.8 is informative on several fronts. You can see that three major business units, Property & Casualty, Life & Disability, and Health, each has the capability to perform claims, administer and bill, make sales and manage customer information. This implies that there are potentially problematic redundancies in these areas that create suboptimal deployment of critical aspects of the business. For example, multiple customer management capability deployments imply that customer information may be being captured and maintained in multiple locations. This situation can lead to the lack of a "one customer" view which can be a key contributing cause of customers leaving the company.

One final issue that Figure 2.8 brings to light is that IT is treated as just another business unit and Information Technology as just another capability from a business architecture perspective. This view of IT as a business unit within the business architecture can be expanded to include capabilities, value stream and business process analysis. When one looks at IT from this perspective, new light may be shed on the level of performance and executive attention that is or should be brought to bear on this critical area.

One final visualization blueprint that is worth considering is the simple cross-reference of business artifacts captured in the business architecture knowledgebase. Figure 2.9 depicts a simple cross-reference report that shows which business units have certain level one and level two business capabilities.

Business Unit	Capability (Level 1)	Capability (Level 2)
Health	Claims	Claim Processing
		Claim Adjudication
		Claim Payment
		Customer Data Update
Life & Disability	Claims	Claim Processing
		Claim Adjudication
		Claim Payment
		Customer Data Update
Property & Casualty	Claims	Claim Processing
		Claim Adjudication
		Claim Payment
		Customer Data Update

Figure 2.9: Business unit mapping
to capability level one and level two mapping

The reporting is a reflection of how this information has been organized in your knowledgebase. For example, if the knowledgebase incorporates a second level of business unit decomposition, such as a Health Claims business unit, to a level two business capability, such as Manage Claim, then you can represent more detailed business unit capability mappings. This is very useful when attempting to get down to the next level of root cause analysis and roadmap planning.

There are numerous other visual representations that can be derived as required from the business architecture knowledgebase, as long as the knowledgebase has been properly designed and deployed. We will incorporate into later discussions as appropriate. When a business architecture knowledgebase has been incorporated into the situation analysis and strategic planning activities within your enterprise, the business architecture team can bring an entirely new and refreshing degree of transparency to the executive suite and management planning table.

Shifting From Operational to Strategic Dashboards

Organizations are realizing that the battle for improving their performance has shifted away from being solely focused on operational improvement. The ability to synchronize various initiatives to provide a coordinated drive toward delivering new capabilities is the new competitive focus. A business architecture framework that is established as part of a strategic planning process can lay the basis for the development of the business architecture knowledgebase. That knowledgebase feeds the business architecture dashboard and the dashboard provides real-time visibility into the alignment of existing efforts within an organization to help reduce the wastage typically found within misaligned, cross-functional initiatives.

Determining how to make use of a business architecture framework, knowledgebase, dashboard and related visualization capabilities is an exercise unique to each particular organization. Typically this process will involve integration with the process which controls the initiation and operationalization of strategic initiatives within the organization. The analytical frameworks that are part of this process reflect product or company differentiators as well as capabilities and priorities, and provide the rationales and measures of benefit for the various initiatives that the organization decides to undertake.

The relationships between the organization's top-level objectives, the analytics used to direct and control the selection of strategic responses and the lower level objectives established as a result of this effort, all combine to form a business architecture knowledgebase that can be useful to foster increased alignment and visibility within an organization.

Management's periodic review of its strategic plan should leverage all aspects of the business architecture framework to produce the supporting analytics on a multitude of in-progress initiatives while helping to plan a multitude of other efforts. This approach provides a way for the organization to rapidly revisit changes in market forces that might cause the organization to re-evaluate its existing objectives.

In addition, in the event that the organization has encountered a failure of its results to meet expectations, this knowledge-base allows executives to quickly evaluate the root causes of that failure and correct it. This approach illustrates how business architecture allows you to both facilitate the understanding of how the organization reached the objectives it is pursuing, as well as supporting the process of tracking progress toward long-term strategic plans.

References

[1] Beatty, Carol A. "Living Happily Ever After . . . with an Acquisition." *Industrial Relations Centre, Queens College*, 1999: 9

[2] Atkinson, William. *Purchasing.com.* April 6, 2006, http://www.purchasing.com/article/224807-Chevron_leverages_buyers_in_outsourcing_decisions.php

[3] Petroski, Henry. *To Engineer is Human: The Role of Failure in Structural Design*

[4] Dr. Lee Lowery, Jr., P.E. *View of the 4th floor support beam, during the first day of the investigation of the Hyatt Regency walkway collapse.* Released into the Public Domain by Author, 1981

[5] Lessons About the Structure of Finance, Chapter 2, Section 3B, Thomas, W. Downs, 2005, http://aohs.ua.edu/cm/fi302/lecturevideos/Lecture3/C2_3B-Overview_of_the_Dupont_decomposition.html

Three

Building the
Business Architecture Team

I cannot think of it this way. It is too big, too complex, with too many work-
ing parts lacking visible connections.
—Lewis Thomas, *The Lives of a Cell*

One major challenge facing organizations launching a business architecture effort is how to best organize a team or teams of business architects. There are a number of options and approaches when it comes to establishing a business architecture team or "center of excellence" and quite a variety have been exercised in practice. In this chapter, we outline various team deployment options that have been used in corporations and government agencies, provide guidance on the pitfalls and benefits of each approach, and share a best practices deployment model that you can use as a guide to setting up a business architecture team in your organization.

As we discuss the creation of the business architecture team, you will want to keep a couple of thoughts in mind. First, various approaches to team organizing, which may be considered suboptimal by one organization, may be the ideal for another organization because a given approach aligns well with political and governance structures. There is no single, ideal approach, but some approaches are preferred from a best practices perspective.

Also keep in mind that the initial governance structure you select may not be the one you ultimately settle on in the long run. We have seen organizations start by using one approach and shift into a more appropriate structure later. In fact it is not unusual in large organizations to find that multiple approaches are being used simultaneously. You do not have to have a perfect solution at the start, but are better off getting some sort of team in place so that you can lay the groundwork for business architecture within your enterprise. The true test, as we discuss throughout this chapter, will be the team's ability to provide visibility into horizontal business challenges and solution strategies that no individual business unit could address effectively on its own.

The Business Architect

We begin the discussion of how to organize business architecture teams by discussing the role of the business architect. In our experience, the most important attribute to look for in a business architect is the ability to see the "forest for the trees" and still be able to drill down into enough detail to understand each tree. Consider, for example, the multitude of issues facing a given business. Management requires insights into structural issues, functional interdependencies and cross-silo redundancies to understand the best ways to plan and deploy various business initiatives. Large-scale, cross functional challenges include issues as diverse as cost consolidation across business units, portfolio analysis of product offerings, bringing transparency to customer interactions across multiple lines of business and portfolio funding analysis. In addition, business areas involved with these requirements often have already begun modeling business processes or have launched IT related solutions. This broad range of interconnected issues is exactly what characterizes the types of problems that organizations are turning to business architecture to address.

It's commonly the case that the business architect is engaged only after heated management meeting debates have gone around in circles and ended in a stalemate. This situation typically stems from having multiple executives from individual business units visualizing the situation and potential solutions from only a single vantage point and not from an enterprise perceptive. It may also be the outcome of taking too deep a dive into various processes or systems without being able to visualize the whole. Either way, initiatives either never get off the ground or individual project teams are overwhelmed by overlapping or disconnected views of the problem, lost in detailed views of process diagrams, spreadsheets, Visio drawings and rambling narratives. Proposed solutions often do not articulate the issues at a level where it can be tied to horizontal business value propositions or the cross-functional, cross-disciplinary business impacts of that solution. This is the world that awaits the business architect.

The business architect must be able to assimilate all of this information and multiple views and discard irrelevant information, uncover hidden factors, represent conflicting structures and tie it all back to the pressing management issue or issues at hand. The view of the problem and potential solutions must view the issues in aggregate, from a horizontal perspective, taking work in progress initiatives already trying to address the issue into consideration as well. The business architect must be able to help executives visualize the root cause of the problem as well as various proposed solutions – all while sidestepping political landmines along the way.

With these requirements in mind we can now identify some of the skills that we would expect a business architect to possess. It is important from the outset to recognize that not every business architect requires in-depth knowledge of every topic area. A typical team might have a senior business architect who focuses on management communications and visualization, strategic planning support and roadmap development. Other business architects might have supporting skills required to streamline architectural views, enhance the knowledgebase, develop visualizations and metrics, and communicate with IT. Additional business architects may be well versed in a particular line of business. Below is a list of the core skills that business architects will need to possess to effectively support a business architecture program within an enterprise.

- Ability to communicate with business professionals and business executives, understand their requirements and help these individuals visualize the root cause and potential solutions to priority business requirements.
- Capacity to help the business assimilate and visualize complex and possibly conflicting information in ways that can hide or expose the details when and where required.
- Knowledge of organizational culture and governance structures needed to adapt and refine business architecture best practices.
- Knowledge of business capability, organizational governance, value stream, business process and business semantic representations needed to facilitate the mapping, aggregation, decom-

position and visualization of current and target state views of
the business.

- Creative capacity to evolve and customize business architecture
  metrics and visualizations to support value proposition related
  objectives against performance.
- Ability to customize repository templates needed to establish a
  business architecture knowledgebase to enable the collection,
  aggregation and decomposition of business artifacts.
- Capacity to communicate and collaborate with IT application
  and data architects as required for business and IT mapping,
  strategic planning and roadmap creation.
- Organizational and governance skills necessary to sustain a viable business architecture capability within the enterprise.

One of the skills described above is particularly important
and addresses the ability to provide executives with visual views of
the business and related issues in ways that executives can readily
understand. Executives do not want, nor do they need, all of the
details that the business architecture contains just as the captain of
the Titanic in our Chapter 1 example did not need to know how
to design a ship. Executives require streamlined, sanitized views of
capability models, value chains, information structures and governance structures that convey just enough information to see the
source of the problem (i.e., the as-is view of the business) and solution options (i.e., to-be options). Synthesizing all the available
information into a cohesive viewpoint, aligned to tell a story as it
relates to critical issues at hand, allows executives to more readily
assess the situation and make decisions. This is a critical part of
the role of the business architect.

What are signs that a given individual may not be an ideal
business architect? This is more difficult to determine but here are
some clues. If a person cannot see the big picture or think holistically, this individual is likely a poor candidate for business architect. If an individual can only think in terms of detailed business

processes, as opposed to holistic business architecture models that tie together many representations and disciplines, this candidate is likely a poor choice for business architect.

Finally, the individual that cannot communicate with management, jumps to solutions before defining the root cause of the problem or sees everything from an IT perspective should not be a business architect. Note that this last point does imply that business architects have no need to communicate effectively with IT data and application architects. This skill is important and every business architecture team should have someone who can communicate intelligently with the IT architects.

The Business Architect vs. the Business Analyst

Because there is confusion between the role of the business architect and the role of the business analyst, it is important to contrast these roles. The vagueness of the business analyst's role is reflected in the industry definition which states that "a business analyst analyzes the organization and design of businesses, government departments, and non-profit organizations; they also assess business models and their integration with technology." [3] While this is essentially the role that the business analyst plays in practice, the way in which they perform this work, who they report to, the techniques they employ and the scope of their responsibilities vary dramatically – even within the same organization.

The difference between the business architect and the business analyst is a matter of intent, breadth of coverage, disciplines employed and on-the-ground realities. Business analysts rarely leverage the architectural disciplines we introduced in Chapters 1 and 2, typically have business unit or divisional constraints on their domain of analysis, and, in practice, almost always focus on gathering and developing requirements for IT. Business architects also engage IT, but this is done from an architectural perspective and within the context of strategic business alignment.

The business architect is renaissance-like, a Polymath with the ability to simplify extreme degrees of complexity in a way that helps everyone understand the issues and concur on workable solutions. Above all, the business architect must be able to not only see the forest for the trees – but help others see that same forest in ways that make sense to them and help them do their jobs more effectively. Assuming that the business architect serves in the above defined set of roles, the question then arises as to the most appropriate governance structure for organizing and deploying business architects.

Business Architecture Center of Excellence

A center of excellence is defined as "a place where the highest standards of achievement are aimed for in a particular sphere of activity." [1] A business architecture center of excellence (COE) then would be where the highest standards of achievement are aimed for or achieved with respect to business architecture. It follows then that the basis for establishing a COE for business architecture rests on the premise that business architecture delivers cross-functional, cross-disciplinary transparency to the enterprise and such an endeavor, by definition, requires a central point of collaboration. It further follows that any discipline with a high degree of strategic importance should have a centralized focal point for best practices adoption, customization and deployment.

Note our emphasis on collaboration versus a command and control structure – which is commonly employed in daily operations or on funded initiatives. Neither the business architect nor the Business Architecture COE is in a position to dictate policy or solutions. As a result, the COE must leverage industry best practices and organizational knowledge to effectively deliver business transparency, support business analysis and planning efforts, and collaborate with all relevant and affected parties as required to deliver bottom line business value. An inability to collaborate will doom the Business Architecture COE because the resulting analysis and proposed solutions will be piecemeal and poorly articulated, resulting in the COE losing its credibility and charter.

Some individuals have argued that it doesn't matter if you call someone a business architect or if the discipline and the team is called a business architecture team, as long as that team provides value to the executives and managers engaged in planning and deployment activities. We challenge this premise because business architecture is a distinct discipline that the vast majority of organizations have not capitalized upon. One could take this line of thinking to an extreme and eliminate all descriptive terms for all roles, divisions, lines of business and other delineating governance structures. The result would be that no one would know where to go or who to collaborate with for a given issue and, even worse, there would be no center of expertise for various skill sets. This is what would happen if business architecture was not used to label the community of individuals that focus on business visualization and transparency. Without such focus, business teams would additionally lack a clear understanding as to where to obtain best practices, supporting literature and related tools to further their work in the area of business architecture.

While some organizations have replaced the term "center of excellence" with words such as "team," "committee" or "group," the importance of stating that the group is focused on "business architecture" remains a constant. The bigger and more common issue is where such a group should reside and to whom should it report. A number of options regarding this question have been deployed in practice, but they typically fall into one of two categories. Should we deploy business architecture within the business or should we deploy business architecture within IT?

Business Architecture COE Accountability & Ownership

In our experience, the inability or unwillingness for business to assert control over the business architecture function has tended to undermine the effectiveness of the core premise of business architecture: to provide transparency to the business based on business-driven issues and demands. If the business does not initiate the Business Architecture COE, it typically results in others taking on the business architecture role. When this occurs, it leaves business architecture in the de facto hands of IT.

We have found that when IT owns business architecture, the focus is almost exclusively on helping IT determine business requirements for IT initiated projects. In this scenario, the business takes a back seat while IT drives initiatives and budgets, which in turn mutes the true potential of business architecture. When considering the option of having business architecture reside within IT, it is important to view the limitations and pitfalls inherent in this approach from a variety of perspectives.

As a general rule, the IT-based business architect reports to an IT controlled enterprise architect and, ultimately, to the Chief Information Officer (CIO). Accountability in all cases is to IT and not to the business. Accountability drives motives and resulting actions. Goals for the IT-based business architecture will be set by IT executives. When the IT-based business architect goes in for a performance review, the IT executive performing the review will expect that the goals set by IT will have been met by this employee. If these IT-specified, IT-oriented goals have not been met, then this employee will be told to either meet future IT-specified goals or move on.

Consider a scenario where the business architect and the Business Architecture COE reside outside of IT. When the business owns business architecture, the nature of the work assigned and the role of the business architect itself begins to shift dramatically. The business-based business architect focuses on issues that are a top priority to business executives and managers because the business is setting this person's goals and will hold the business architect accountable for achieving those goals. The business-based business architect is intent on understanding and bringing transparency to the root cause of priority business issues and crafting business-specific solutions. IT related solutions are a potential byproduct of these efforts, although there may be times when no IT engagement is even warranted.

In stark contrast to the IT-based business architecture scenario, when the business has responsibility for business architecture, the business sets the agenda of the Business Architecture COE. For example, ask IT how to best address a situation where customers are unhappy because they get different answers to the same question from different business units. In this example, customers may be moving to the competition because communication with an enterprise has become so onerous. IT will likely propose technical solutions such as a data warehouse, an enterprise service bus, middleware technology or new systems – without understanding the root cause of what is driving customer losses or business solutions.

Now reverse the situation and take this same problem to a business-based business architect. The proper response involves mapping customer centric capabilities, value streams, underlying business processes and information to relevant business units as a basis for assessing the root cause of the problem and communicating this root cause to the executive team. Upon analysis of the situation, the business architect crafts a view of the to-be business architecture based on the strategic changes requested by these same business executives and then assists with creating a business transformation plan.

Business architects may also engage IT data and application architects to incorporate IT related factors into the analysis and projected options and solutions. The degree and depth of IT engagement vary based on the situation and may be quite limited if IT is a non-factor in the scenario. Either way, the analysis and proposed solutions are focused on directly addressing priority business requirements – not IT requirements.

One story comes to mind when we find organizations that ask how they can move business architecture into the business when there is no infrastructure in place to house such a center of excellence. One day, corporate IT executives at a financial institution told one of their senior IT employees that they were now in charge of business architecture. This person's first move was to request a transfer into the business so that he could more effectively deliver on the needs of the business. This is where he now resides as he begins his journey to establish a business architecture team. We give this advice to business architects who feel "trapped" under the IT enterprise architecture umbrella. There is a way out – transfer into the business.

In practice, IT frequently owns the business architecture function. In other cases, business architecture may be scattered across numerous segregated business units. In certain cases, both of these situations are true. Depending on where your organization falls in this range of scenarios, there are varying approaches for creating a cohesive and effective business architecture team that can work with disparate business units and IT toward a common set of solutions.

Commonly Applied Business Architecture Organizing Concepts

A variety of business architecture organizing concepts are applied in practice. Approaches range from the haphazard to the highly structured. To gain an historical perspective, we have provided an overview of several team organizing options we have seen in practice along with the pros and cons of each approach.

IT-Based Business Architecture Team: Situating the business architecture team within IT is a common approach that is based on the evolution of the enterprise architecture (EA) team, which has historically been focused on IT architecture topics. Prior to the introduction of business architecture into an enterprise, a typical EA team is likely to have been divided into three or four groups that would include technical architecture, data architecture, application architecture and, possibly, security architecture. The security category is also found outside the EA team in many cases. IT determined that it required better insights into the business and this decision resulted in the creation of a group of business architects who report to the head of EA.

Business architects deployed under the EA team generally focus on delivering business requirements for funded or planned IT initiatives. Some of these IT-based business architects have made a significant effort to position themselves within business units, understand business issues and collaborate with business professionals. Their focus, however, largely remains on flushing out requirements for IT related projects and not on providing the transparency required by business executives and managers who need to understand and resolve a host of pressing business challenges. The upside of this deployment approach is that the business architects typically have a strong collaborative relationship with the application and data architects. The downside is that the business architects are, at the end of the day, servicing an IT master and not the business and this undermines the very pretext for business architecture.

The Business Unit, Business Architecture Team: Business architecture teams have evolved within line of business specific divisions, agencies and departments. These teams are generally constrained to working within a given business unit, although they do collaborate with other business units and with IT. These business unit teams have the capacity to fulfill basic business architecture functions, but only as far as the business architecture reflects a given business unit. If the business unit is self-contained and does not share customers, business partners, capabilities, processes or information with other business units, this approach can offer good deal of value to that business unit. If, on the other hand, a business unit shares common customers, partners, capabilities, processes and information with other business units, then the business architecture will reflect an incomplete and potentially misleading view of the business.

A business unit specific team can serve a useful purpose in this second scenario if the team coordinates with other business units through a centralized Business Architecture COE. The central COE sits outside a given business unit and has a horizontal view of the enterprise. We will explore the central COE concept further in the section discussing the ideal business architecture organizational structure. The biggest downside of the business unit specific team is that divisional executives will continue to apply silo-based solutions to enterprise level issues and this will result in the funding of piecemeal initiatives in situations that require holistic solutions.

We must emphasize that silo-based solutions to horizontal challenges are not only the norm in many organizations, but are commonly reinforced through funding and budgetary models, management decision making structures and ingrained culture. Even organizations that have successfully established a centralized COE continue to fall back into silo-based decision making and solution deployment approaches. When this happens, it further compounds many of the challenges that enterprises are trying to address through business architecture in the first place.

In practice, the multi-divisional COE approach has been used at large diverse financial institutions and has had some interesting implications and challenges. A large bank, for example, had grown through a series of mergers. Various business units continued to function as independent entities under a single corporate umbrella. The bank's situation is characterized by significant business capability, business process and information redundancies across an overlapping client base. Essentially, this was the result of having never completely assimilating business models that were absorbed as a result of these mergers. Unfortunately, the bank continues to struggle with consolidation and cost reduction by placing the burden on a fragmented IT organization.

The interesting aspect of Business Architecture team deployment at the bank was the degree of inconsistency across various divisions. One division had its business architecture team within IT while others did not. Either way there was no coordinating COE and, therefore, business architecture efforts were constrained to offering silo-oriented solutions when they should have been delivering horizontal support for the enterprise. There is a silver lining in this story. In spite of the fragmented business architecture team deployment that exists across the bank, it is better positioned from a business architecture deployment perspective than a bank that has no business architecture team infrastructure. The fragmented team deployment is not ideal, but can also be viewed as a transitional phase on the journey to establishing a centralized Business Architecture COE.

The Free Floating Business Architect: The "free floating" business architect has no team structure or COE to work through or coordinate with and is, therefore, on their own to service their respective business units. This situation is likely the first step in an organization's path to establishing business architecture. Many of these business architects were probably business analysts at one point and someone decided that they should be business architects because the concept of business architecture was gaining industry recognition.

Deploying business architecture through free floating, loosely coordinated business architects is virtually impossible and one can make a good argument that these individuals are not really serving in the role of a business architect but are actually business analysts. A single individual could comprise a COE, which is how many of these groups start out, but it is more likely that business unit managers are using these individuals to research business requirements and coordinate with IT on those requirements. While this is a valuable service, it does not fall under the definition of a business architect.

The Independent Enterprise Architecture Team: This rarely employed yet viable approach involves moving the entire EA function, including the business, application, data and technical architecture teams, totally out of IT and out from under the control of the CIO. Such a team would have a Business Architecture COE that reported up to a VP of EA. While this offers independence from IT that one would desire of a Business Architecture COE, it does raise the question of the wisdom of moving essential technical, application and data architects outside of the IT domain. The upside here is business architecture independence from IT while the downside may be the risks and challenges of separating critical enterprise architects from their home within IT. This clearly falls under the category of "whatever works best for your enterprise is the approach to use" and this approach has been used in practice.

The Independent Business Architecture COE: The independent Business Architecture COE is a team that has horizontal views of the enterprise, is not beholden to any single business unit or special interests, and is independent from the IT organization. The role of the independent COE is to bring the full breadth and depth of business architecture best practices to bear on horizontal business challenges as deemed appropriate by the executive team. This group also collaborates with business unit specific business architects and teams and works very closely with application and data architects from the IT EA team. This structure, which we view as ideal, is discussed in more depth the next section.

Ideal Business Architecture Organizational Structure

The ideal or classic alignment of business architecture within an enterprise should place the Business Architecture COE in a neutral role, with as much access and insight into horizontal business requirements and strategies as possible. The ideal structure is reflected in a centralized enterprise-level Business Architecture COE that has direct access to the executives setting and funding cross-functional, high priority business issues. The COE should have similar access to business units through business unit-specific business architects and to IT through data and application architecture teams. Figure 3.1 depicts the organizational alignment and governance structure of a classically defined Business Architecture COE along with relationships between other business and IT architects within the enterprise.

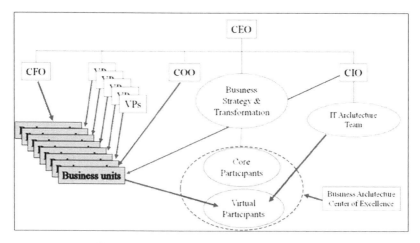

Figure 3.1: Business Architecture COE:
A best practices governance structure

The governance structure in Figure 3.1 is instructive on several accounts. First and foremost it represents an independent, Business Architecture COE comprised of core participants and virtual participants. The core participants are the keepers of the best practices, knowledgebase, visualization techniques, scenario libraries, solution templates and collaboration skills. This team, even within a Fortune 500 company, should not be excessively large. Several large, multinational corporations have Business Architecture COEs that range from 5-7 core participants. The name of the game in business architecture is collaboration. A COE's ability to coordinate and leverage the architects, analysts, executives and subject matter experts that outside the COE will ultimately determine the effectiveness of the overall business architecture program.

Figure 3.1 also provides us with the governance and reporting structure for the centralized COE. While the head of the team, typically a senior manager, reports to a senior VP, COO or even CEO, the Business Architecture COE itself takes direction from a cross-functional team of senior business executives.

The Strategy and Transformation Team shown in Figure 3.1

represents a group of executives, typically called a steering committee or an executive committee, that deal with strategic, high priority business issues. Challenges, such as the customer consolidation scenario we discussed in Chapter 2, cannot be solved by a single division, business unit or individual because the root cause of the problem extends beyond the control or domain of any single group or executive. The strategy team or executive committee is the main customer of the business architecture team.

Whether you choose an organizing model that resembles the one pictured in Figure 3.1 or select a different approach, the true test of any COE is the ability to have access to executive planning teams that require root cause analysis, solution options and input to various roadmaps to address complex horizontal business challenges. In order to do this, executives require a core team that they can rely on to apply the best input possible on key issues through the use of best practices-based business architecture.

Other than coordinating executive communication, dissemination of best practices, knowledgebase management and blueprinting techniques, there is one other role the centralized Business Architecture COE plays. It ensures continuity of the community of practice for business architecture across the enterprise. We previously discussed how the business analyst's role in many organizations is that of a chameleon – morphing into whatever it takes to survive. This has happened to business unit-based business architects at some organizations because they have no shared principles to guide their practice.

The COE establishes and disseminates these principles to ensure continuity of practice and sharing of best practices. This is essential because working on horizontal initiatives requires coordination across business units, regions and disciplines that may have little or no shared history. Shared principles streamline cross-functional collaboration, serving as a foundational set of commonly agreed upon truths that guide a business architect's practice regardless of location or reporting structure.

The Agile Business Architecture Engagement Model

As requests for assistance with priority, cross-functional business challenges are received and processed by the COE, small teams must be able to rapidly assemble to perform research, gather information, enhance the knowledgebase with this information, produce views of the current state business architecture and develop relevant metrics and related visualizations. The team will additionally be called upon to draft variations on the target state business architecture based on proposed solutions, assist with strategic roadmap development and collaborate with IT architects as appropriate. These engagement teams are normally comprised of selected core team participants, business unit-based business architects, subject matter experts and, as required, IT data and application architects.

Note in Figure 3.1 that each business unit, as well as IT, has virtual representation within the COE. Virtual representation is defined as participation in a group, team or initiative that does not reflect your formal reporting structure. For example, a business architect from each business unit may collaborate on a project to determine the root cause and recommended transformation options needed to address a loss of customers, spiraling operational costs or business partner coordination issues.

Figure 3.1 also depicts the IT architecture team's role within the Business Architecture COE. The virtual role played by IT architects is focused on data architecture and application architecture related issues. As a rule, if IT architecture analysis, mapping and target state transformation work is required as part of a given Business Architecture COE initiative, the COE will want to engage the application architect and data architect at the appropriate juncture in the assessment. From a virtual team perspective on a given research effort, this may be at the moment the engagement team is formed. The Business Architecture COE engagement model breaks down as follows:

- The executive or steering committee or strategy team identifies a priority initiative that requires research from a cross-functional perspective.
- Core team business architects examine the issue and determine which business units or other groups need to be engaged based on a capability and organization unit mapping as defined within the business architecture knowledgebase (assuming it is in place).
- Core team members engage business architects in various business units to join the initiative.
- If there is an IT mapping or transformation factor involved in the analysis, core team business architects engage an application and data architect in the research effort.
- Subject matter and third party experts are added to the team based on overall requirements and recommendations from the business unit-based business architects.
- A collaborative team is established for the life of the research and planning effort.
- The collaborative team is accountable to the executive committee or strategy team that initiated the inquiry.

Business architecture engagement teams must assemble rapidly and, therefore, should not be bound by traditional long-term funding and cost justification models. To accommodate this agile engagement model, the executive steering committee governing the COE will need to establish annual funding for horizontal initiatives to ensure that engagement team deployment for various research efforts can move forward quickly. Virtual participants from various business units can then tap into this funding structure on an engagement by engagement basis. The COE is ultimately responsible for managing this centralized budget, which should be established annually by the Steering Committee in conjunction with the COE.

Business architecture engagement deliverables include metrics, current and target state architectural views, a business transformation strategy and supporting roadmap. The strategy and roadmap reflects a synchronized view of business and IT transformation. The engagement team, through the COE, delivers the results of a given engagement to the steering committee and other executives as required. Implementation is driven by the appropriate steering committee, engages various business units and IT executives as required.

As implementation planning progresses, the engagement team can help identify relevant parties that need to be engaged in a given solution based on the transparency produced through its analysis. At this point, the engagement team's role winds down and the COE then takes over the role of providing the steering committee with point-in-time blueprints and metrics as the current state business architecture evolves into the target state. We should make it clear that while the COE can help track transformation progress and facilitate roadmap clarifications, it is not an implementation team. Project deployment goes through the teams that would typically align processes, transformation user interfaces, refactor applications and perform various other tasks in conjunction with any major initiative.

The Multi-Divisional COE Organizational Structure

Establishing and leveraging the Business Architecture COE within a multi-divisional or multi-agency environment that already has pockets of business architects or teams deployed can be challenging. Many times, as in the aforementioned banking example, an organization has multiple business architecture deployments. While this may look like a significant challenge first, the situation actually can open up the door to greater enterprise transparency while creating opportunities for cross-functional collaboration. Figure 3.2 depicts a governance structure and organizational view of the central Business Architecture COE in an enterprise that has multiple COEs established across various business divisions.

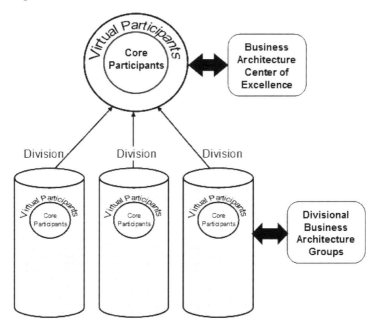

Figure 3.2: Business architecture governance structure
with federated COEs

In the governance structure depicted in Figure 3.2, each division or business unit typically has a complex business environment that requires independent COEs to evolve business architecture views for that division or business unit. In this scenario, each division or business unit is led by a senior executive with independent profit and loss responsibility. In some cases, each division is autonomous enough to warrant independently produced views of the business architecture. This would be true, for example, where a multinational holding company has a healthcare unit, large appliances unit, aerospace group and other independent businesses. In this case, there are no shared customers and only shared reporting at the holding company level.

More often than not, however, the business units or divisions in question are somehow tied together with shared customers, common value streams, information and capabilities. In this case, the enterprise as a whole requires aggregate views of these business units to address complex challenges such as creating a single source of truth for customer information, aligning customer change management activities or even consolidating down to common deployments of business capabilities such as wealth management or customer support. This is where a central Business Architecture COE becomes essential to the long-term success and viability of the enterprise.

The difference between the situation depicted in Figure 3.1 and the one in Figure 3.2 is the degree of autonomy of each business unit and the fact that each unit has its own independent Business Architecture COE. In Figure 3.1, the business architects within each business unit are free floating personnel within that unit who serve in the role of contributor and recipient of business knowledge maintained by the central Business Architecture COE. In Figure 3.2, the relationship is similar although more formalized and each COE is likely to have its own independent knowledgebase and domains of practice.

A situation such as the one shown in Figure 3.2 can arise in a number of ways. The most common scenario, however, involves a large enterprise, that has grown through mergers and acquisitions, where divisional executives have determined that they each require a business architecture solution. As we stated previously, this opens up an opportunity for greater transparency and collaboration than could be achieved through a top-down deployment of a central Business Architecture COE.

A major benefit of having a centralized COE includes the ability to consolidate a knowledgebase into a common, high-level view of the business architecture. This assumes the deployment of federated knowledgebase repositories unique to each division or business unit. A federated or divisional knowledgebase would have the capacity to store more extensive and more granular business knowledge. For example, a divisional knowledgebase may include detailed business process mappings while a centralized knowledgebase would not track every process. The ability to create a roll-up view of the knowledgebase within the central COE, however, creates the unique capacity to support visualization and analysis across the enterprise that federated knowledgebase deployments cannot support.

The additional value of having a central Business Architecture COE along with divisional COE deployments is the ability to gather and share business architecture best practices, scenario templates, metrics, terminology, knowledgebase structure and tooling. A collaborative governance structure, explained at the end of this chapter, is essential to ensuring that such sharing occurs. Under this framework, the centralized COE coordinates the assimilation and dissemination of best practices and the alignment of core business architecture principles and role definitions.

Before we discuss the best ways to leverage federated COE deployments, we must offer words of caution for anyone encountering a multiple COE scenario. Situations like this are often fraught with political entanglements driven by the belief that a given area needs to guard and protect their business knowledge. Each division thinks it is totally unique and is locked into this belief structure. This mindset challenges fundamental business architecture principles, which we will discuss in the next section on collaborative governance. One point that should be clearly and frequently communicated to appropriate management teams and business executives in these situations is that horizontal challenges cannot be addressed by applying silo-based thinking that is promoted and institutionalized when no centralized COE exists.

When multiple, federated COE structures emerge in your enterprise, you can apply some basic techniques for organizing a central Business Architecture COE in a multi-divisional enterprise with federated COEs. The following guidelines generally apply:

- Identify horizontal issues that executives have been wrestling with that would be virtually impossible for a single division to address. One example includes synchronizing customer or other shared information across silos.

- Determine which, if any, projects are either planned or underway to address these issues. Review the viability of IT-driven (versus business-driven) solutions and silo-based solutions.
- Meet with as many Business Architecture COE representatives as possible to determine if they are encountering similar issues or have management support to strike up a collaborative effort that would identify root causes and proposed resolutions.
- Begin collaborating with one or more COEs on issues where there is benefit in working collectively to accomplish tasks that could not be completed independently.
- Document successes as you go so that management can gain an understanding as to the benefits of having a central point of collaboration across business units, Business Architecture COEs.

Note that the approach outlined in the above guidelines is not a top-down approach. We have, rather, opted for a bottom-up organizing approach that allows the collective COEs to build upon successes within their own business units. The bottom-up COE may not have anyone to report to, which may challenge traditional management thinking. This is not necessarily problematic given that it represents an evolutionary stage of business architecture maturity. In this case, the COE exists solely as a creation of business unit or divisional COEs. To ultimately succeed, however, there must be recognition and sponsorship of the centralized team by a horizontal executive steering committee.

In order for this bottom-up COE deployment concept to function effectively, a set of principles must be established and adhered to by participating business unit COEs. The key principle should state that any issue that cannot be effectively addressed by a given COE engages other COEs to collaborate on a sustainable, horizontal solution. We outline basic principles to support this type of governance structure later in this chapter under the section on Collaborative Governance.

One challenge in a large organization is that you may not know where, how or who is serving in the role as a business architect. This is the ultimate irony because business architecture is focused on transparency. To address this issue, one financial institution created a Business Architecture COE Intranet site to attract other business architects from across the enterprise into a central COE. This was the brainchild of one of the divisional COE leaders, and it was a very successful way of triggering a self-organizing business architecture effort.

It may take some creativity to align forces across multiple COEs, but the key driver for this is the demand for solutions that can address cross-functional challenges that cannot be solved by an individual business unit. If this demand exists and the executive team is driving the need for solutions, then multi-divisional alignment of COEs will be motivated to happen.

Collaborative Governance:
Teaming with Business Units, IT
and External Entities

We have mentioned the concept of collaborative governance several times within the course of our discussion on establishing and governing the Business Architecture COE. Collaborative governance is defined as "an endeavor in which deliberation and decision making are disseminated to the individuals who, collectively, are most knowledgeable *and* most capable of participating in and enacting a particular decision." [2]

The benefits of adopting collaborative governance may not be immediately obvious from the definition, but the concept is essential to establishing and deploying business architecture – whether federated COEs are deployed or not. The characteristics of an organization that adopts and deploys collaborative governance concepts are listed in Figure 3.3.

There are important several considerations referenced in Figure 3.3 that are important to the establishment and the success of business architecture in general and the COE in particular. These factors include transparency, cross-functional collaboration, self-organizing teams and the gravitation to centers of excellence. All of these points are foundational to the success of business architecture and particularly important to the establishment of a COE.

❏ Enterprise governance structures are transparent and readily accessible to business professionals at every level of the enterprise.

❏ Management seeks to create cross-functional, cross-disciplinary teams to fulfill enterprise strategy and goals.

❏ Business units responsible for common or overlapping functional capabilities seek to collaborate to further enterprise strategy and goals.

❏ Business professionals are free to self-organize at any level for any purpose to further enterprise strategy and goals.

❏ Governance structures facilitate the natural gravitation of business professionals toward creating and participating in centers of excellence.

Source: The Role of Collaborative Governance in Business Architecture, William Ulrich, Cutter IT Journal, March 2008

Figure 3.3: Characteristics of organizations
that practice collaborative governance

Consider, for example, the issue of transparency. The previously discussed financial institution had multiple Business Architecture COEs that lacked fundamental transparency. As a result, it had limits to its ability to address cross-functional challenges, particularly where it involved common customer and product strategies. The idea of cross-functional collaboration is essential in any horizontal initiative as we discussed in our customer consolidation example in Chapter 2 and collaborative governance makes this possible.

Self-organizing teams will be explored further when we discuss business and IT alignment in Chapter 4, but the concept is based on an attribute of successful organizations that has all but been lost in today's highly segregated enterprise. Consider what would have happened if Airbus project engineers from France would have contacted Airbus engineers from Germany in the Airbus case study we cited in Chapter 1. The disaster that befell Airbus might have been avoided. We have built so many barriers, however, between business units, between the business and its customers, and between business and IT that even simple communications either take too long or just never occur because of the bureaucratic walls that we have built up over the years.

Finally, gravitation toward centers of excellence should be a natural human tendency but the tendency has been bred out of our corporate DNA. When given a task or facing a challenge, such as addressing the need to more quickly put products into the market, a given business unit tends to pursue this as a solo effort. Little consideration is given to the benefits of a collaborative effort, to the questionable value of tackling such an initiative in the absence of other business units or even to the fact that another business unit may have already deployed a solution in this area. If the organization is lucky, two employees may stumble over the fact that there are multiple initiatives going to improve product deployment abilities in different business units, but even corporate culture will likely prevent them from speaking up about this issue.

This is the same corporate DNA that resulted in the proliferation of standalone Business Architecture COEs at the financial institution discussed earlier. A center of excellence, by definition, should be at the center of the enterprise with the ability to engage at the peripheral. The centralized Business Architecture COE, whether created through the concepts outlined in Figure 3.1 or in Figure 3.2, is based on a collaborative governance model that begins to reprogram this DNA at a very basic level.

Organizing the Business Architecture COE is not command and control driven but a collaborative endeavor. The very reporting structure of the COE to a steering committee reinforces this notion. The reason for this is that the Business Architecture COE and the business architect rarely have formal command and control authority. There are those in the industry that promote the business architect as a command and control figure but in reality, this is not the case. Therefore, business architects and the COE itself must adopt a collaborative governance mindset where governance is driven by purpose, principles and social networking structures versus command and control structures.

In order to introduce and begin to disseminate the concept of collaborative governance, business architects can leverage a standard framework for organizing collaborative governance structures that is called the "Six Lenses on Organization." [4] This framework introduces six common sense views of an organization and includes purpose, principles, role definition (participants), organizational structure, constitution and practices (feedback loop). While establishing a written constitution is optional, although valuable, understanding the basic purpose, shared principles, role definition and organizational structure is essential to all aspects of business architecture.

The two most basic concepts to collaborative governance are the purpose of a team and the principles that guide it. A purpose is the answer to the "elevator question." If an executive asks you what you are working on, you need an answer that can be stated before that executive reaches his or her floor. When you say that you now work in the Business Architecture COE, you will likely have only seconds to tell the executive what this means. This is your purpose. A sample purpose for the business architecture team could be stated as follows.

Provide enterprise transparency to facilitate problem analysis of priority, cross-functional business challenges and assist with developing strategies to resolve those challenges.

At the heart of collaborative governance are the principles that guide actions. A principle is defined as "basic generalization that is accepted as true and that can be used as a basis for reasoning or conduct." Principles guide actions but do not tell someone how to do their job. Consider some selected sample principles for a Business Architecture COE and for the business architect:

1. Major, funded initiatives should be undertaken only with the appropriate degree of transparency of all aspects of the busi-

ness affected by or affecting that initiative.

2. A business viewpoint of any issue is essential in diagnosing the root cause and developing the related action plans needed to resolve critical business issues.

3. Business units and individuals are committed to engaging in business initiatives as necessary to ensure the success and delivery of those initiatives.

4. Initiatives engage technology professionals that have a stake in a business capability or process affected by or affecting that initiative.

5. There will be open exchange of information and ideas with business and technology teams as is required to identify the root cause behind and resolution of critical business initiatives.

6. All blueprints, knowledgebase deployments, ideas, concepts and plans are open to all participants unless this violates privacy or security

7. Knowledge collected on a given business architecture analysis effort is captured and reflected in the business architecture knowledgebase as appropriate to the use of that knowledge on future initiatives.

8. Business architecture concepts, methods, knowledgebase, metrics and tools will consider industry best practices as appropriate to the success of a given initiative.

These are only a subset of sample principles for a Business Architecture COE but these examples provide you with an understanding of the value and the ability to create your own principles. For example, say that the executive committee is reviewing an initiative involving the consolidation of credit card processing across divisions to a single outsourcing supplier and they engage the Business Architecture COE to help. Principle #1 would suggest that every division and department with a credit card processing capability would need to be engaged in this effort. In addition, transparency must be brought to bear on all related information and processes within those divisions and departments.

The actions of the business architect and COE are always tested against fundamental principles. The strength of the principles, which would need to be developed collaboratively with the business architects within the enterprise, is that any business architect, regardless of the business unit or COE that the person reports to, has a set of principles to guide their actions. In addition, your actions are guided by principle – not politics.

Role definitions, another aspect of the Six Lenses, are not new but are commonly missing in many enterprises. There can be sub-roles for the business architect but it is important to have a common definition for the business architect that can be shared across COEs and business units. If the role of the business architect is not concisely defined, then the discipline and the value of the enterprise will not be sustainable. Consider the following sample role definition for the business architect.

The business architect provides business transparency as required to facilitate collaborative solutions to business challenges.

The sub-role definitions inherit this definition, but go into more depth as far as knowledgebase management, tool related skills, visualization capabilities, executive communication and other areas. We will revisit the issue of collaborative governance in later sections of this book, particularly as it supports business and IT alignment in practice.

In summary, establishing the Business Architecture COE is an important step in the evolution of business architecture within your enterprise. Take care, however, not to force business architecture concepts on the executive team too quickly. You should wait until you have established a foundation for your efforts and identified opportunities and situations where business architecture can support critical initiatives.

Organizations have made the mistake of trying to obtain too much funding, building too large a team and blueprinting too much of the enterprise at one time without tying the business value being delivered directly back to executive priorities. You are better off taking cautious steps than attempting to take on too much too soon and without demonstrating value along the way. Otherwise, the Business Architecture COE could be gone before it has a chance to make an impression.

References

[1] Center of Excellence Definition, Encarta, 2010, encarta.msn.com/dictionary_1861694214/center_of_excellence.html

[2] "The Role of Collaborative Governance in Business Architecture," William Ulrich, Cutter IT Journal, March 2008

[3] Wikipedia, Feb. 2010, http://en.wikipedia.org/wiki/Business_analyst

[4] "Chaordic Design Process: Six Lenses on Organization," www.chaordic.org/cd_process_activities.html

Four

Business Architecture and IT Architecture Alignment

Fools ignore complexity. Pragmatists suffer it. Some can avoid it. Geniuses remove it.—Alan Jay Perlis

You just completed an executive walkthrough of your analysis of the customer management consolidation issue initially raised in Chapter 2. You provided executives with a visual walkthrough of the challenges you are facing with regard to the many access points and business processes associated with customer updates. You discovered that customer information is not viewed consistently by various business units, each of which considers customer management to be a capability that is unique to their business unit. Now, management understands the business issues and is interested in solutions, but much of the current environment is automated. While you have a handle on how to proceed from a business perspective, it is unclear as to how IT can and should fit into this transformation effort. Thus begins the cycle of business and IT alignment.

A Business-Driven Approach to Building IT Architecture Strategy

The above scenario begins where most business and IT alignment journeys should begin – with a priority business issue that requires an action plan and resolution. This is not to imply that every issue is strategic or a top priority – the business determines ultimate priorities with IT. Yet business and IT architecture alignment is essential to identifying, funding and sustaining solutions for the enterprise – and this is where business architecture plays an important role.

But just how does business and IT alignment (architecture alignment is implied) differ from what has historically been happening in traditional IT planning and deployment efforts? First and foremost, the business assesses the situation from a business viewpoint prior to jumping to an IT-centric solution. This business-centric approach requires assessing cross-functional implications, educating executives on the impacts and crafting solution options that allow business to dictate the timing, funding and value proposition of proposed solutions. In the customer management consolidation example, transparent, horizontal analysis led to the determination that the way in which the company was managing customer information and customer communications was deeply flawed.

IT implemented this flawed business model and evolved it over a period of decades. In other words, the IT architecture enabling the business is a reflection of the business and all silo-based requirements that have driven the evolution of underlying application and data architectures. Undoing this flawed business model is not a job that IT can or should undertake on its own because IT typically takes a technology-based perspective. If the business drives the initiative, however, and bases its analysis on a comprehensive understanding of the root cause of the problem, the opportunities for achieving real value increase dramatically.

The business team must take proactive and ongoing ownership of efforts such as customer management consolidation and other priority initiatives. All such initiatives, from planning through various incremental deployments, must be informed by the transparency delivered by the business architecture. With a solid knowledge of the root cause of relevant challenges from a business and an IT architecture perspective, the business is well-positioned to drive collaborative business and IT solutions to address those challenges. Ultimately, the success of business-driven initiatives requires that business and IT craft a phased deployment roadmap of cost justifiable solutions that incrementally deliver value to the business at each step of the way.

Aligning Business and IT Strategy through Business Architecture

Ensuring that your business strategy drives IT architecture transformation requires "synchronized business and IT alignment." Today, phased synchronization of business architecture and IT architectures is the exception – not the rule. Either business or IT is continually attempting to shift the enterprise toward new goals, but progress that is rarely achieved because business and IT goals and strategies are out of sync. This, in turn, creates a lurching effect where one side is trying to force transformation upon the other side, which is invariably unprepared for the impact of such a transformation.

Consider many of the mergers that occurred over the past decade. Business decisions to acquire or merge with other companies drove enterprises into a situation where redundant infrastructures, capabilities and business processes were consolidated under a single enterprise. In most cases, IT has yet to consolidate backend application and data architectures, choosing instead to create frontend facades and backend data warehouses to create the illusion of alignment. But even these frontends were ill conceived, deployed by individual business units with little regard for a holistic view of the customer or other stakeholders. Piecemeal, silo-based solutions were used to address consolidation and integration issues that should have been addressed through a horizontal, cross-functional approach.

In addition to backend IT challenges, many business units operate as isolated entities relying on unique, customized business processes. It is never fair to say that either IT or the business was solely responsible for preventing the smooth transformation of a given company into a seamless enterprise. In some cases, the strategic funding model for certain business units or the enterprise as a whole means that there is no clear approach for creating and funding a common vision of an integrated enterprise. In other cases, the business itself may not consider consolidation in line with corporate strategy.

Many times, however, the lack of transparency as to the root cause of major business challenges related to mergers and acquisitions leads to the inability to craft solutions. This same lack of transparency blinds executives to the fact that the business is suffering as a result of structural redundancy and fragmentation. If you doubt that this situation is commonplace, examine the IT architecture of any large enterprise that has undergone one or more mergers. Most of these organizations still have separate applications and databases that have been patched together in a variety of ways. IT may be whittling away on piecemeal solutions to replace a system or create some sort of enterprise service bus ("ESB") that may help a given business unit, but the consolidation issue as a whole is being ignored.

While business and IT misalignment stifles enterprise agility, the situation is typically compounded by the fact that various factions within the business and within IT are out of sync with each other. In many post-merger environments, mirror image business units continue to support customer management, billing, order processing, procurement, claims, credit card and a host of other business capabilities.

For example, IT executives at a healthcare insurance provider had plans to consolidate multiple product lines and business units within the IT architecture. IT executives presented a strategic view of an integrated business and IT architecture as the basis for a scenario-based transformation strategy and roadmap that they could deliver over a period of time. When IT executives met with senior business leadership to layout various scenarios, the business team rejected the business unit consolidation idea almost immediately. For a variety of reasons, business leadership did not or could not envision a unified business model void of redundancies. The business continues to run as two individual companies to this day.

The lessons learned from the health insurance provider scenario serve as a guide to business and IT leadership when attempting to establish an alignment strategy. First, attempting to drive business and IT consolidation from the IT side of the house challenges the basic principle that IT strategy should be business-driven. In the above example, business executives took offense at the idea of an IT executive pushing for business unit consolidation. The ultimate lesson learned was that, if IT attempts such a foolhardy move, it is best to shut that notion down as soon as possible – not after you have spent $50 million of the company's money, which, by the way, happened at this company

Another lesson learned was that there is the truth in the age-old adage that a picture is worth a thousand words. It took less than half an hour to convey what IT had in mind using a simple set of high-level blueprints. Senior business executives could quickly determine that they did not share this vision. While the senior VP of IT felt that the meeting was a failure, we felt that not wasting an additional $50 million on another quixotic quest was a victory for the enterprise as a whole. The most important lesson learned in this case was not by IT but by the business. Business leaders were forced to weigh the pros and cons of business unit consolidation – and they chose to leave things as they were. We note that senior business leadership opted for the status quo in spite of repeated warnings that a third or fourth merger would result in increased operational costs, redundancy, inefficiency, lack of customer integration and instability.

The Business - IT Communication and Language Gap

Business people and IT people do not speak the same language in terms of how they view the world, communicate issues and address problems. It is often said that IT needs to have a better understanding of business issues. We hold out little hope that this is going to happen because IT professionals often lack the background needed to do this and generally focus on IT goals, not business goals. It has also been said that business people must have a better grasp of technical concepts. We know this will not occur because business professionals do not have the time, inclination or need to become IT savvy.

And no, the ability to master Excel by a frontline business professional does not equate to being able to understand enterprise information systems and complex data and application architectures. The business professional knows his or her own job and understands what is in front of them. With a little help, they can suggest how to improve their own role through technology. IT must capitalize on this knowledge and these abilities. On the flip-side, gaining insight into how IT professionals view the business as far as their role in impacting IT requires examining statements and actions. Here are three statements that summarize what at least a few IT professionals feel when it comes to the role of the business professional in major IT projects:

- "We know what's best for the business and we will tell them what they need." [Statement from a Chief Information Officer (CIO) at a large, international telecommunications firm]
- "If only business people would learn UML, then all of their problems would be solved." [IT architect on how business could communicate more effectively with IT]
- "No, you don't want to talk to the business users." [Well known IT architect and industry commentator when asked how to best go about determining project requirements]

This communication issue, while endemic to many IT cultures, can be overcome through a variety of ways. These include creating a business-driven approach to addressing critical business requirements, moving decisions that should be made by the business back into the business and having business executives and professionals reclaim the role of establishing strategic transformation roadmaps. We address the cultural issues through engagement models in Chapter 6. Positioning the business as the strategic driver of transformation strategy relies on our ability to extend business architecture transparency to IT architecture, business and IT dependencies and business and IT transformation strategy. This process begins by bringing transparency through business architecture to major IT spending initiatives and investments.

Refocusing the Enterprise on Business-Driven IT Strategy and Investments

Shining a spotlight on IT investment strategies exposes the depth and breadth of the gap between business and IT. In Chapter 1, we discussed the failures associated with IT-driven solutions, including studies citing wasted IT investments and related project failures that organizations have endured over the past two decades. Continuing to base funding strategies on IT-driven, IT-centric responses to what IT "perceives" as business issues will continue to drive up the number of failed initiatives and wasted investments.

This last issue is significant because money is pouring into IT projects, many of which are being capitalized over a period of years. As discussed in Chapter 1, in just one year, $160 billion of IT project investments were considered wasted. [1] Organizations must reverse course and turn IT investments into business value. This can only be done, however, if the business steps in to reclaim ownership of these investments. Business architecture provides transparency into business issues and resolution options and into the impact of the projects being funded to achieve those resolution options. Fundamentally, business architecture provides a vehicle for the business to refocus its investment strategy on business specific, bottom line benefits.

The first place to start a business and IT alignment effort is to assess how IT consumes investments within an organization. When we review planned or "in flight" IT initiatives, it is surprising that the stated benefits are almost exclusively IT-centric. This typically tells us that IT has "sold" the project to the business as a solution that will allow IT to deliver future value more quickly and more effectively. Consider this following list of "business benefits" taken from several IT project charters:

- Ability to use less senior programming and analyst expertise on the system
- Cheaper hardware costs
- Improved systems performance
- Improved ability to maintain the system
- Having a system that is now written in Java (versus COBOL)
- Reduced maintenance costs

- Improved time-to-market
- Better user experience

These "supposed" business benefits were taken from the *cost / benefit analysis section* of multi-million dollar initiatives for major IT projects that were either underway or in the cost justification stage. The first six "benefits" are clearly of value to IT while the last two are at least somewhat business-centric; although we have seen IT organizations mean IT change request turnaround when they say "time to market." A business professional would expect this term to mean improving the ability to deliver new products and services to customers. The last item on the list, "better user experience," is incredibly vague and is typically included in IT benefit lists as a catch all to satisfy business units funding these initiatives.

While hard to fathom, IT commonly sells the aforementioned examples to the business as business benefits. Rarely does one find items on the list such as lowering operational costs within our call center, reducing the time it takes to put a new financial instrument in the field or allowing customers to change information and gain immediate notification that the change occurred across every product line. Benefits such as these do show up occasionally, but more often than not IT is focusing on IT-centric benefits and goals.

Business executives have even started using IT-centric cost justification terminology. We ran into a senior VP at a healthcare insurer that parroted IT-centric benefits back to us when we asked what the business was hoping to achieve from its $40-50 million, multi-year investment in a set of new systems. The executive told us that the new services oriented architecture (SOA) would provide significant time-to-market value to the business – once the system was fully deployed. We doubt that this individual could provide even a cursory overview of SOA and would be challenged to tie tangible business benefits to this project.

Whether it's SOA, Cloud Computing or the often promised,

large-scale replacement project, IT always has a new silver bullet solution it can use to ensure that major initiatives continue to get funded by the business. There are those within the IT industry, primarily on the vendor side of the business, that figure if IT keeps promising some slightly out of reach, technological Nirvana, the business will continue to fund massive, IT-driven and IT-centric projects. These projects continue to burn through increasingly scarce capital and resources. Business executives must put a halt to the funding of major initiatives based on IT-centric benefits that cannot be tied to priority business requirements.

Changing the Tide: Establishing a Business-Driven Transformation Strategy

Over the past 25 years, IT has undergone countless changes and revolutions. We have seen a wide variety of computing languages arrive on the scene along with new methodologies, modeling techniques, design and development tools, computing standards, hardware, project management disciplines and Holy Grail architectures such as SOA and Cloud Computing. In spite of all of these new tools, modeling techniques and methodologies, IT has virtually lost the ability to create new, enterprise level software systems – certainly on any reasonable scale.

One might argue that there is a wealth of software development going on, but most of this work is being done to either add new software to the stack of business applications already in place or to make small maintenance changes to older systems. Old databases and file structures are almost never substantively modified and neither are the core enterprise applications that access and update this data. These enterprise applications are comprised of order processing, billing, material tracking, inventory, trading, claims, accounting, policy management and a wide variety of other business systems that comprise the core of an organization's computing ability. Much of it is written in a language called COBOL, which is over 50 years old, but numerous other languages abound.

None of the above should really be considered a problem from a business perspective. Why should the business care if software is written in COBOL, unless the money being spent on IT initiatives is not delivering bottom line business value? This is not a slight toward IT because in most cases the business has sat idly by while these projects continue to churn away, eating up scarce resources and delivering limited business value. Business professionals have taken some recent positive steps. For example, business process management (BPM) has been useful where it has been effectively deployed, but it has also complicated the situation because IT has co-opted BPM as an IT requirements vehicle in lieu of truly understanding the capabilities and information requirements that current and new technology deployments must enable and support.

The industry is now struggling with getting BPM synchronized with SOA while ignoring the rest of the business architecture and IT architecture. We have seen major initiatives spend several years mapping out to-be business processes. These processes were then handed to systems integration teams as "business requirements" with the expectation that these integration teams could just whip up a set of viable replacement applications. These teams were told to build SOA solutions from little more than a mountain of BPM diagrams that were not supported by information models, organizational models, capability mappings or value stream analysis for the current or the target business architecture. These projects failed – in rather dramatic fashion in some cases. Other similar projects continue to limp along on life support.

The reason for these failures, which continue unchecked in many organizations, is that there was no understanding of the current state business architecture or no understanding of the current state IT architecture. As a result, there was no phased business and IT transformation plan and no plan to address the reuse or phased deactivation of the installed base of application systems. So much was left off the table in terms of analysis and planning for most of these projects that only a giant leap of faith can explain how business executives could unleash tens of millions of dollars funding on these initiatives.

In order for the tide to change regarding wasted investments in IT initiatives, the transparency that we have insisted upon with regard to business architecture must be extended to IT architecture to ensure that business-driven IT initiatives can actually be delivered and business value can be achieved. Extending business architecture transparency into IT architecture enables phased, synchronized transformation of the entire enterprise ecosystem.

In addition to business and IT architecture transparency, business and IT need to reengage as true, collaborative partners so that business-driven goals and objectives extend into IT project funding and accountability. Business architecture shifts the role of the business in transformation initiatives from passive observer to active motivator, driver and participant. We discuss collaborative engagement models for business transformation in Chapter 6 and focus on business and IT architecture mapping and transformation mechanics in the remainder of this chapter.

A Quick Primer on IT Architecture

Before discussing how to synchronize business and IT architecture transformation, we must provide a little background on the term IT architecture. IT architecture establishes a blueprint of the application, data and technical architectures that currently comprise or will comprise information technology deployments that support the business.

Figure 4.1 depicts the three traditional aspects of IT architecture along with a fourth category – shadow systems. Each of the four aspects of IT architecture work in consort to enable various business capabilities and automate business processes.

Data architecture is a blueprint of the data structures that business professionals rely on to run their business. Application architecture provides a blueprint of the application systems, services and software related IT aspects that deliver business functionality to business professionals and customers. The technical architecture is the blueprint of all platforms, languages, operating systems, security systems, middleware and supporting technologies required to deliver a functioning IT environment.

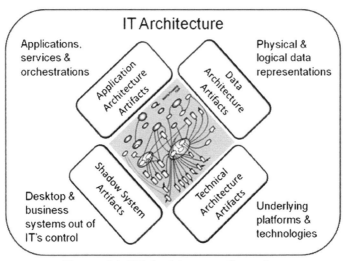

Figure 4.1: IT Architecture Overview

The application architecture is the most visible aspect of IT architecture to the business. Application systems automate the vast majority of business capabilities in a given enterprise. Many of these applications, however, date back decades. As important as they are, older application systems rarely provide the ideal level of support for business capabilities and related processes. Application systems have fallen out of alignment with current business requirements because many application architectures are based on how the business functioned several decades ago. If this is not the case at your organization, you are a rare exception. A simple test you can perform to assess the degree of misalignment between business and IT is to determine the degree of manual and desktop workarounds the business has created to get through an end-to-end business process. In many cases, manual efforts and desktop systems support more than half of a given process because the application systems automating these processes have fallen behind where the business is today. The degree of business and IT misalignment increases proportionately to the number of manual and shadow system workarounds and such misalignment creates severe strategic and tactical disadvantages.

The data architecture is an essential yet rarely discussed topic. Business professionals care about information – not the vehicle that was used to deliver that information. They want accurate, timely, synchronized information when they need it and in the form that is most conducive to business intelligence and operational effectiveness. While many people are typically involved in gathering, formatting and reporting on business data, very few people are involved in transforming the underlying architecture that houses the business data. Data management is an activity that tends to be done through the rear view mirror and business can suffer for it.

Data is updated, manipulated, reorganized, aggregated and even fixed outside of the scope of the core data architecture. If you doubt this, count the number of spreadsheets and desktop databases a given business unit is using. Other signs of data architecture being out of sync with the business are tiered data warehouse deployments, large groups of analysts assigned to creating "customized" business reports and extensive executive and compliance reporting performed by business units and not IT. Data architecture is the core of the IT architecture and, when misaligned with business information requirements, organizational effectiveness, efficiency and compliance suffer. All of this can contribute to lost revenue, compliance issues and audit violations.

Finally, the technical architecture can be thought of as the wiring and plumbing that runs through a building, ship or city. Unless you build and maintain the technical architecture, your interest in it as a business professional should be limited. While we recognize that IT is maintaining aging or obsolete technical architectures that may need to be upgraded or replaced, justification for these projects must demonstrate a clear business case. Ultimately, the technical architecture only enables the data architecture, application architecture and shadow systems that directly service business professionals and these last three aspects of IT architecture are the focal point for business and IT alignment. Multi-million dollar projects based solely on technical architecture migrations must undergo serious review and business justification. (Note: We are not challenging the value of Web 2.0 or other advances; we just want to tie them to business value.)

Shadow systems represent business-developed software that typically resides on desktop environments, hidden from IT's line of sight in the "shadows" of the business. Shadow systems support numerous critical business capabilities across an enterprise, yet do not exist as far as IT professionals are concerned. Consider the executive reports, business intelligence or operational roles processed and supported by Excel, Access or more sophisticated tools. These spreadsheets, databases and other programming tools augment manual tasks and weaknesses in the data and application architectures. We have even encountered shadow systems running in more sophisticated environments, including business-maintained servers and mainframe systems that remained long after IT had attempted to centralize IT architecture. The term shadow system is used to mean *any* business-owned, business-maintained software not under IT stewardship.

Each of the four legs of IT architecture plays a key role in providing automation support for various business capabilities and business processes while housing the real world business information that a business needs to make decisions and maintain ongoing operational continuity.

Visualizing IT Architecture
from a Business Perspective

In Chapter 1, we discussed how business architecture establishes a blueprint of the enterprise as a means of providing transparency into various aspects of your business. Using this blueprint, executives, managers and other business professionals can readily identify the root cause of critical business challenges, shine a light on resolution options, craft commonly agreed upon strategies and establish a path forward based on facts – not speculation and conjecture. Organizations must extend this level of clarity to encompass a view of the business as it is supported by and intertwined with IT architecture.

Views of IT architecture that come from IT are generally expressed using technical representation not readily understood by business professionals. One such category of representations used to express IT architecture is the Unified Modeling Language (UML), although other visual representations exist to represent both current state and future state views of IT architecture. UML tends toward a technical representation of IT. As a result, using UML to communicate with business professionals can result in missing the mark. This is particularly true when UML is used as a basis to communicate with executives who have little time and less inclination for learning how these diagrams work.

A second factor that is even more problematic is that many of the IT-created, IT-issue and IT-resolution viewpoints are from an IT perspective when they should be based on business perspectives. Typical IT diagrams omit views of organization units, capabilities, customers, third parties, business information and even business processes. There is little communication regarding how the organization works and an overwhelming emphasis on how the technology works – or how it will work as envisioned by IT.

This last issue involving the architectural views of the "way things will be" versus the "way things are" is the source of many of the greatest missteps organizations tend to make when charting a course forward to address a given issue or series of related business issues. The lack of a shared, well-articulated understanding of the business and IT architecture is the source of many common pitfalls that include:

- No shared basis or understanding to support root cause analysis of the issues at hand

- Inability to determine the scope of analysis required or the scope of changes to be applied to the current state environment
- Lack of visibility into the depth and breadth of impacts on business units, business processes, information and related aspects of the IT architecture
- No capacity to envision a solution that can be delivered with maximum benefit and minimal disruption to the business
- Inability to incrementally deploy a roadmap to lower the risks and increase the odds of success of the proposed solution

We discussed the pitfalls of not having a shared understanding of the business architecture as input to the process of crafting solutions to priority business requirements. These pitfalls are magnified dramatically when discussions begin to move toward funding large-scale, multi-million dollar IT initiatives. More often than not, when a significant business issue is being discussed, the solution typically involves a heavy dose of IT architecture. As a result, IT is pulled into the discussion early and in many cases told to "find a solution" to a poorly articulated business issue. The result is a technical solution that the business cannot understand, costs a lot of money and often misses the mark.

In other words, executives must shift the approach toward business-based analysis that drives business-centric solutions to ensure that near-term and ongoing business value can be achieved. A business-centric approach delivers more robust solutions that have a direct and lasting impact on the business bottom line. In addition, providing a holistic view of the real underlying challenges means that executives are less prone to driving IT toward technical solutions that do not solve the problem.

In addition, the business will be less prone to blindly accepting IT-centric solutions that take a radical, big bang approach, with ROI delivered at the backend of a high risk, multi-year and high cost initiative. These types of projects drive the wasteful spending on IT we previously cited from Standish Group report. A simple view of the horizontal nature of organizations, business processes and supporting application and data architectures provides backdrop for our discussion on business and IT alignment.

Figure 4.2 shows how business units, processes, applications and related data structures are aligned by silos across an enterprise. Political and physical barriers segregate business units, stifling cross-functional communication, collaboration and visibility.

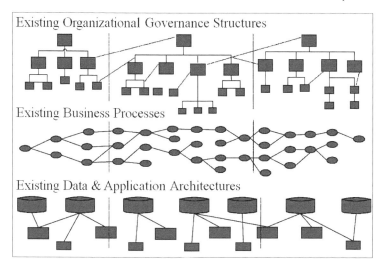

Figure 4.2: Horizontal dependencies of business units, processes, applications and data

Backend IT architecture silos have had a maze of intertwined technologies built on top of them reflecting past efforts to make everything work smoothly. This approach has introduced marginal value to the enterprise. An IBM study found that "recent advances in integration middleware technology have provided some relief by making it possible for financial institutions to move customer information across channels. But in many cases the technology has been laid over flawed legacy architecture and has merely created more duplication." [2] In other words, silo-based solutions have added complexity to backend IT architectures beyond the intent and expectations of the teams that implemented those solutions and the business executives that funded them.

Business unit segregation can be significantly more complex in reality than the depiction in Figure 4.2. Redundancy and fragmentation typically occurs at multiple levels across regional and divisional boundaries. Business units are often matrix-based by line of business delineations and further complicated by regional discrepancies. Organizations that have undergone a merger or an acquisition typically have residual redundancies in deployed business capabilities and processes and these redundancies are mirrored within the IT architecture.

When IT as a business unit is introduced into this mix, the relationships become extremely complex. As a result, issues resulting from or complicated by business unit segregation are sidestepped or bandaged over. While IT has made a legitimate effort to address business concerns, most projects tend to view requirements and solutions from the narrow perspective of that team or business unit. As a result, multiple initiatives deliver piecemeal, conflicting or redundant solutions that cannot be implemented, are rejected by business teams or deliver suboptimal solutions – all the while taking a large bite out of limited budgets. Piecemeal solutions can be tolerated only until the pain and consequences of the situation become unbearable – resulting in customer losses, competitive encroachment, revenue reductions or worse.

Consider our customer management consolidation scenario where the organization set its sights on consolidating its view of the customer. IT-centric solutions for such a scenario typically focus on technical architecture deployments. For example, IT oftentimes puts a diagram in front of the executive team with the term ESB (a technical architecture term) on the chart. Use of this term in an executive session often means that solution architects jumped directly to technical implementation and sidestepped business, application and data architecture considerations. While technical architecture becomes irrelevant at some point, issue analysis based on current state business, application and data architectures must come prior to discussion of technical solutions. Figure 4.3 extends the executive view of the current state business architecture we introduced in Chapter 1, Figure 1.5, incorporating application and data architectures.

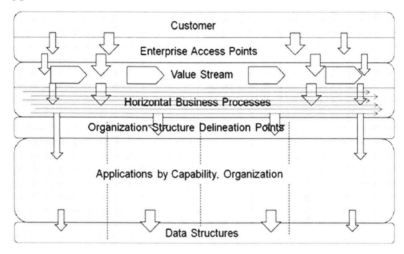

Figure 4.3: Executive view mapping business architecture to application and data architectures

While Figure 4.3 is a highly abstracted view of the current state analysis, it does serve as the basis for executive discussions on why customers end up in multiple places across an enterprise and why it is so difficult to reconcile this information in a meaningful way. Figure 4.3 highlights the fact that multiple business processes implement the same value stream, which fragments and replicates customer information management across numerous applications, shadow systems and other data structures. This executive level view, derived from the business architecture knowledgebase, helps management see that replicated deployments and business processes across business units and product lines further drive application and data architecture fragmentation. Executives can visualize that the challenges facing them are systemic and require well-conceived analysis and strategy.

This executive discussion, in turn, typically triggers working sessions with various business unit directors and, in this scenario, application and data architects. The next level of analysis in this case involves examining the business units, processes, information and related aspects of the business that implement conflicting, redundantly deployed customer management capabilities. This analysis incorporates a mapping to core application and data architectures to the capabilities they support. Figure 4.4 shows an example of a report generated from the business architecture knowledgebase that maps applications to the business capabilities and business units they support.

Business Unit	Capability (Level 1)	Capability (Level 2)	Application Support
Health Claims	Claim Management	Claim Processing	Health Claims System
		Claim Adjudication	Health Claims System
		Claim Payment	Master Claim Payment
		Customer Data Update	Health Claims Systems
Life & Disability Claims	Claim Management	Claim Processing	L&D Claims Applic.
		Claim Adjudication	L&D Claims Applic.
		Claim Payment	Shadow Systems
		Customer Data Update	Shadow Systems
Auto & Fire Claims	Claim Management	Claim Processing	A&F Claims App.
		Claim Adjudication	A&F Claims App.
		Claim Payment	A&F Claims App.
		Customer Data Update	A&F Claims App.

Figure 4.4: Business unit, capability, application mapping report

Figure 4.4 extends business unit-to-business capability mapping introduced in Chapter 2, Figure 2.9, which was limited to the business architecture. Figure 4.4 shows how to extend business transparency into the IT architecture, which facilitates analysis of the customer management consolidation requirements. Customer information is buried inside applications that support other capabilities and value chains. In this case, a customer can change their address at the same time they are making a claim, which is part of the claim management value chain. In addition, these applications automate various claims capabilities and product lines. IT alignment will, therefore, be difficult.

Aligning backend application and data architectures to business capabilities cannot be delivered over the short term based on the analysis of reports such as the one shown in Figure 4.4. This puts significant pressure on planning and architecture teams to craft a solution that delivers near-term value with minimal impacts on IT architectures. There is no quick fix to this situation but steps that can be taken from a business and IT perspective that will address the issue, but require coordinated business alignment.

As we stated in Chapter 1, the analysis leading to the creation of the business and IT architecture blueprints in Figures 4.3 and 4.4 relies on an extended business architecture knowledgebase that includes business and IT architecture mapping. A foundational subset of the conceptual model required to perform the high-level mappings in Figures 4.3 and 4.4 is shown in Figure 4.5.

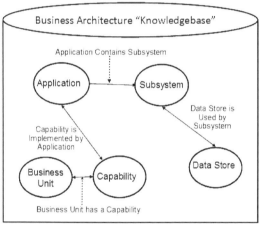

Figure 4.5: High-level, partial business and IT architecture knowledgebase mapping

We have omitted a number of business and IT Items from Figure 4.5 for purposes of clarity. A more comprehensive view would include business unit decompositions for division or departments and a capability and value stream mapping and capability decompositions down to a level two capability. This view, however, demonstrates the power of a simple conceptual model to support strategic initiatives. We used a similar mapping structure to perform enterprise wide business and IT architecture planning for a federal government agency that made billions of dollars of purchases annually. [3]

Additional detail is required within the knowledgebase to support roadmap planning and deployment. This more granular knowledgebase would minimally require mapping the value stream to business, business to the user interface and shadow systems, user interface to subsystems, subsystem to applications, and business information to data stores. Variations or additional information might be required depending on the approaches used or the environment.

Synchronized, Business-Driven Business and IT Alignment

From a historical perspective, business and IT alignment has remained a difficult goal to achieve, typically characterized by brute force mandates to use a new system, the rejection of various commercial-off-the-shelf (COTS) solutions and a bevy of failed projects. Books have been written on how to improve business and IT collaboration and an endless parade of management concepts, buzzwords, and methods have been employed by IT to improve the software delivery process. Unfortunately, the results from a business value perspective have not improved dramatically.

The lack of progress is due to the fact that the vast majority of these disciplines take aim at only one side of the issue – IT architecture analysis, design and development. More recently, management methodologies have turned their focus on business process improvement. But processes comprise only a portion of the overall business architecture, focusing on "how" things are being done within the business. While beneficial, this limited myopic view of business architecture is not enough. Ulrich Homann stated in his seminal white paper on business capabilities that "Traditional business process modeling does not align business requirements with technology structures and investments."[4] In other words, business processes are insufficient as a foundation for strategic planning and business and IT alignment. Accomplishing these tasks requires a holistic view of business and IT architecture interdependencies appropriate to the challenges that need to be addressed.

Business architecture, when mapped to IT architecture, provides the missing piece in this puzzle – allowing business and IT architectures to evolve in synchronized fashion, maximizing value at each step of the journey. Critical business issues, large or small, require business and IT synchronization. This is only possible when management, planning and deployment teams have cross-functional, cross-disciplinary transparency into the current and target state of the business and IT architecture. Figure 4.6 depicts the concept of synchronized business and IT transformation to a target state architecture.

Figure 4.6 shows several important concepts regarding synchronized business and IT transformation. First, the transformation path shown in Figure 4.6 does not imply a one-time journey from current state to target state. Rather it represents the concept of continuous transformation of the business and IT architecture. Under this concept, views of business and IT architecture must undergo continuous evolution to reset those views to reflect ongoing transformation across business and related IT deployments. Each transformation step should have a business-driven aspect to it in order to move the organization to a future state that increases competitiveness, operational effectiveness, customer satisfaction and efficiency, and overall profitability – assuming that this is how your enterprise is measured.

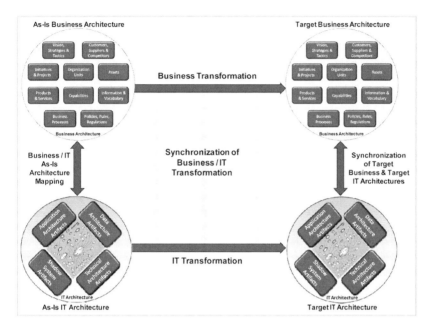

Figure 4.6: Synchronized business and IT architecture
transformation model

A second important concept is that current state and future
state business architecture blueprints allow business and IT professionals to perform root cause analysis, envision solutions, and
perform transformation options, select and refine a strategy, and
craft a roadmap of projects to achieve that strategy. This means
that future state IT architecture does not become an end in and of
itself but rather serves as a means to achieving business transformation. This approach puts business professionals back in the
driver's seat from a planning and funding perspective.

Under this approach, if business executives cannot envision
clear business benefits to IT investments, funding for these investments should be withheld or withdrawn. Note that there is an
argument to be made for the fact that a certain degree of IT infrastructure improvement is required on an ongoing basis. Even
these investments, however, should be viewed from a business
perspective and incorporated into the overall business and IT ar-

chitecture transformation model. Synchronized transformation requires that aspects of IT architecture relevant to various business domains undergoing transformation be mapped to the business architecture within the knowledgebase. Business and IT architecture mapping allows management and planning teams to envision a target state IT architecture that meets priority business requirements and articulate related transformation and options from a holistic perspective.

Current-to-target state business and IT architecture mapping facilitates the creation of a strategy and solution roadmap that business and IT can work toward collectively. This strategy drives subsequently more detailed analysis across the breadth and depth of the business and related IT deployments. This includes, for example, mapping interdependent processes to user interfaces and shadow systems, information to data structures, and business capabilities to applications as a basis for building an implementation roadmap.

Business and IT synchronization is not just applied to strategic issues but tactical aspects of business and IT transformation as well. In addition, synchronizing impact analysis across business and IT can work in either direction and applies to changes large or small. For example, it is not uncommon for a small request to be implemented by IT and have the new "feature" wreak havoc across business processes, spreadsheets and even upstream and downstream applications. This means that even minor issues require synchronized analysis, resolution and deployment.

Revisiting our customer management consolidation scenario provides insights into how root cause analysis and synchronized transformation planning work in practice. Figure 4.7 depicts a consolidated long-term, future state view of business and IT architectures. Specifically, business processes implementing the customer management value stream across multiple business units are consolidated under this future state view, at least to the extent feasible given unique requirements across the business units. This long-term view also envisions a consolidated set of customer management services that various applications can invoke to manage a common view of a customer.

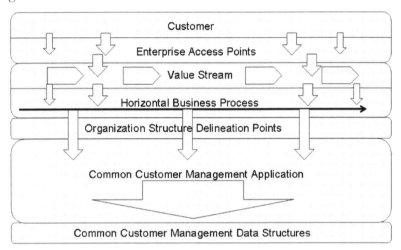

Figure 4.7: Executive view of long-term target state
of customer management consolidation

Recognizing that this long-term view cannot be achieved immediately and that the business has customer management requirements that require near-term solutions is one major benefit of creating a common business and IT vision that the business can fund and business and IT can collaboratively implement. The reality of the situation is that complex, backend application and data architectures do not lend themselves to simple, quick-fix solutions. Visualizing long term and intermediate views of business and IT current-to-target state architecture helps align business's and IT's vision of a phased approach that delivers incremental and long term business value.

Figure 4.8 depicts the current state and long-term target state of the business and IT architecture as it would ultimately need to evolve. Figure 4.8 consolidates the current state view from Figure 4.3 with the target state view from Figure 4.7. In doing so, we have provided a simple view for executives that requested an end-state view of the business and supporting IT architecture.

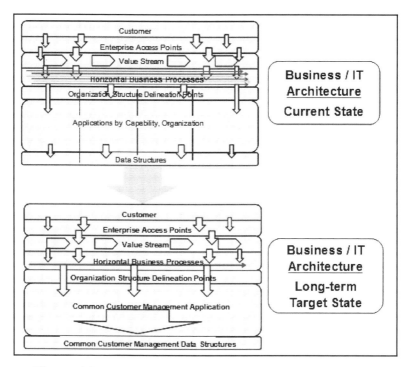

Figure 4.8: Executive view, mapping current to long-term target state of customer management

Given that the long-term target state in Figure 4.8 would require that IT create and deploy a series of common customer management services and modernize application and data architectures across business units and IT silos, management subsequently requested a near-term set of options along with a phased deployment roadmap. In this scenario, such a roadmap requires early stage deployments of "mini-applications" through the use of agile frontend projects that rely on small collaborative teams drawn from business and IT.

Another way to envision synchronized business and IT transformation is by zooming back on the overall business and IT ecosystem. In doing so, we can view IT data and application architectures at the core of a highly automated work environment, with the business on the outside looking in. To the business professional, IT is pretty much a black box. The business professional's view begins and ends with things they can see and touch, such as a user interface or a downloaded data file that can be used for spreadsheet extracts. Figure 4.9 depicts such "line of sight" limitations based on which side of the business and IT architecture you are on.

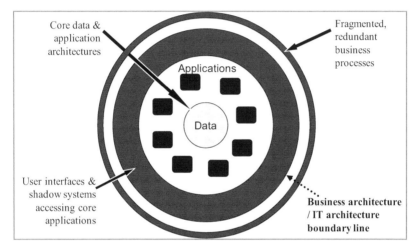

Figure 4.9: Business and IT architecture depicting
line of sight limitations of business and IT professionals

The data and application architectures on the inside of the circle in Figure 4.9 are only visible to IT professionals. A business professional cannot see beyond shadow systems while the IT professional lacks visibility into business processes, terminology and shadow systems. Teaching the business to "speak IT" is counterproductive because business professionals already have full-time jobs. Business professionals do, however, have expertise in their area of the business and understand that small improvements can have a dramatic, positive impact on their ability to perform their jobs.

Working directly with the frontline business professional is an excellent way to understand requirements and concurrently create incremental business value. Face-to-face communication between frontline business professionals and IT professionals focuses on visible projects that deliver the most business value in the least amount of time. These agile projects, which should align with priority objectives, also offer insights into mid-term and long-term roadmap deployment that ultimately moves the enterprise toward a consolidated view of the customer.

Agile projects with frontline professionals address the number one cause of problem projects – inadequate understanding of requirements. The lack of requirements knowledge is the number one reason for project failures. [5] IT has gone through Herculean efforts to employ standards, tools, methodologies and an army of business and IT analysts to resolve this problem, but the challenge of understanding requirements remains. Agile, frontline-driven solutions facilitate synchronized business and IT architecture alignment by tackling the requirements issues head on.

A collaborative, agile approach, working closely with frontline professionals, goes well beyond traditional business process modeling - and for good reason. As Homann told us, processes are not a solid foundation for strategic business and IT alignment. Yet, IT continues to rely on process analysis as a basis for delivering software requirements. Sole dependency on business process analysis for IT requests has been responsible for the unsuccessful deployment of IT modernization projects. A holistic approach is much more effective. [6].

Collaborative, agile projects streamline and automate fragmented, convoluted processes, interwoven with manual steps, shadow systems and backend user interfaces, incrementally moving the enterprise to consolidated customer views. This tactile concept is based on the recognition that the reality of what is going on in the business is unique to a given subset of frontline professionals and direct engagement is essential to addressing priority business requirements. Focusing on small, achievable and ROI-driven solutions through frontline user engagement aligns with the concepts of limiting the span of comprehension and the span of control for any given initiative.

Studies have shown that the larger the project, the more likely it is to fail. According to the Standish Group, large projects fail more often than small projects. "Only 3% of projects that cost $10 million or more succeed." [7] Larger projects drive up the required span of comprehension and span of control, which increases the odds of failure. Reduce the span of comprehension and the span of control for business and IT professionals to deliver business solutions and you concurrently cut the time it takes to deliver business value, the risks involved in taking on these projects and the odds of failure.

Agile projects should tie back to business strategy. In our customer management consolidation scenario, business executives prioritize aspects of the customer management value stream to be addressed as a top priority and establish a roadmap of small projects that derive the greatest benefit in the shortest timeframe. Collaborative teams of business and IT professionals consolidate and automate business processes at appropriate points within the value stream and through deployment of mini-applications that replace manual steps, aging user interfaces and shadow systems. These highly agile, frontline-driven solutions facilitate business and IT architecture alignment where it delivers the most value to the customer near-term in weeks or months – not years. From a strategy perspective, the view of the current and intermediate target state of the business and IT architecture using this approach is shown in Figure 4.10.

The transformation strategy associated with these views involves small deployment teams, streamlining and automating one set of processes at a time and creating a baseline mini-application that can then be deployed across business units and processes until consolidation is achieved. This transformation process is phased across business units with each phase involving a small number of focused frontline users working with agile design and development personnel to deploy increasingly more sophisticated mini-applications.

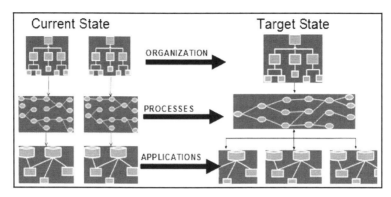

Figure 4.10: Current state and intermediate target state views of consolidated business unit and front-end architecture

Make no mistake, this is not the traditional "lipstick on a pig" deployment. These are business-driven solutions that result in intelligent mini-applications that ultimately result in the target state view to the right in Figure 4.10.

This approach aligns frontend customer change processes and backend customer notification processes across business units and product lines. Solutions include new customer interfaces as well as internal frontline user facilities across each business unit. The benefits gained are significant in terms of customer perception. Customer change requests, which traditionally lack transparency, are now traceable across business units and deployment views. The value stream lifecycle that used to take months is now reduced dramatically, with operational efficiencies achieved at each stage of the journey.

This approach has been proven in practice, delivering near-term value while providing IT with an increasingly sophisticated roadmap for evolving backend applications. A case study from TELUS Communications demonstrates the power of this approach. In a 2008 interview with BPM Strategies Magazine, TELUS's Juanita Lohmeyer discussed the value of such an approach. The concept, which employed rapid response teams across the organization, was called the "Quick Win" approach.

According to the interview, Quick Win [8]:

- "Is based on a series of small projects that deliver profound improvements to the TELUS business community from an operational improvement perspective"
- "Focuses on immediate tangible business value that fuels passionate business engagement"
- "Applies technology at the speed and level of understanding of the business"
- "Delivers continuous evolution as business requirements mature"
- "Supports transformation by collaboratively solving current problems while exposing opportunities for growth"

The concept deployed at TELUS replicated solutions resembling the target state view shown in Figure 4.10 many times over through the use of small teams deployed across business units and regions. The interview stated that the solutions were "profound" and that technology was applied at the speed and level of understanding of the business. Quick Win delivered a five-to-one return on investment to TELUS [9] and continues to be deployed.

Architecture-Driven Modernization and Business and IT Transformation

While going after high-value business solutions through the rapid deployment of mini-applications at the frontlines of the business is a powerful concept, this approach alone is not enough to meet strategic business and IT alignment requirements. At some point, core application and data architectures need to be aligned to accommodate business strategy.

Later stages of our customer management consolidation scenario exemplify why core IT architecture modernization is ultimately required. While the rapid response approach to business and IT alignment addresses many priority requirements through the deployment of mini-applications, success is constrained by continued reliance on backend, silo-based applications and data structures. Under this scenario, there is typically a stated goal to achieve a single source of truth from a customer, regulatory, audit and business perspective. Even though frontend customer information is rationalized across business units, processes and mini-applications, the customer data represented in various applications and stored within backend databases and master files remains inconsistent and fragmented across product lines and business units.

In addition, business intelligence and the actual updating of customer information is likely to be delayed by fragmented application architectures that continue to stymie product line consolidation and various customer initiatives. Executives must determine the return on investment of modernizing core application and data architectures, but they should do so with an understanding that there is an alternative to the traditional rewrite of existing systems or COTS replacement options that can tend to take years and cost tens of millions of dollars. The alternative is architecture-driven modernization.

Architecture-driven modernization is defined as "a collective set of tool-enabled disciplines that facilitate the analysis, refactoring and transformation of existing software assets to support a wide variety of business and IT-driven scenarios." [10] This IT capability is not commonly thought of as the first option when considering how to meet strategic business requirements that require core IT architecture transformation. Yet there is a long history of modernization success stories, documented in formal case studies. [11]

Modernization of IT architectures involves the analysis, refactoring and transformation of those architectures as determined by any number of scenarios that business and IT choose to pursue and fund. The important point to remember is that IT has options when it comes to backend, large-scale IT architectures. Figure 4.10 depicts an easy way for business architects and business professionals to think about this concept when engaging IT.

Figure 4.11 represents the concept of continuous business

and IT architecture transformation from several perspectives. Technical architecture transformation provides minimal business value and business engagement. Application and data architecture transformation, however, has a more direct impact on the business because these architectures house business information and automate the processes and rules needed to optimize business performance. Transforming application and data architectures, as the "horseshoe" in Figure 4.11 suggests, should be undertaken from a business architecture-driven perspective, which can dramatically increase the value of a modernization initiative.

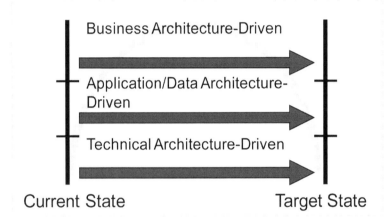

Figure 4.11: Business and IT transformation
enabled through architecture-driven modernization [11]

Business executives, managers and architects are not expected to understand the inner workings of complex application and data architectures. But neither is it sufficient to hand off accountability for ensuring that IT architecture transformation remains synchronized with business architecture and business strategy. It is quite clear as to what happens when business abdicates responsibility for business and IT alignment: $160 billion in wasted IT investments in just a single year according to the Standish Group study. [12] So what can the business do when it lacks the expertise needed to establish a business and IT architecture transformation roadmap? We recommend the following:

1. Educate executives on the risks of failed approaches to IT-driven alignment strategies. Standish Group, among others, has published studies on the failure rates of large projects.

2. When discussing IT investments, ask about the risks and inherent failure rates associated with traditional rewrites and COTS deployment projects.

3. Ensure that there is adequate consideration for existing IT application and data assets in any business and IT alignment strategy that requires changes to or replacement of core application and data architectures.

4. Verify that IT application and data architects have a basic knowledge of architecture-driven modernization. In any medium-to-large IT organization, application and data architects should have a working knowledge of modernization concepts.

5. Engage outside expertise to advise you on options when making large-scale IT investments. This does not imply blindly handing millions of dollars to a systems integrator, but does suggest engaging sound advice when it comes to IT investments.

6. Demand that IT architects engage with business architects to build target state views that are business-friendly. (If you cannot understand a concept, you should not have to fund it.)

Long-term business and IT alignment options typically involve establishing capability-centric SOA services and retooling application architectures to facilitate the incremental modernization of core application and data architectures to leverage those services. In our customer management consolidation scenario, this involves incremental deployment of the following steps:

1. Deactivation of core application architecture functionality for any capabilities now contained within newly deployed mini-applications.

2. Standardization and redesign of data architecture to align with newly deployed mini-applications, which represent previously

synchronized views of custom information.

3. Deployment of centralized data architecture for customer information as appropriate to the business and applicable IT business units.

4. Identification and consolidation of customer management capabilities across all application architectures currently supporting those business capabilities.

5. Deployment of common business services by IT to manage customer information from a centralized perspective.

6. Refactoring of applications to access common customer management services and deactivation of application functionality that currently supports these capabilities.

7. Phased deployment of these modernization stages across all relevant applications.

The timing, phasing and approach to the above modernization scenario would vary based on business-driven cost justification and IT architecture complexity. The approach could be phased in over a long window of time, or teams may choose to move more quickly. The business architecture knowledgebase continues to evolve to reflect changes as they are deployed. This approach could also serve as the catalyst for the eventual modernization of entire applications, based on the need for the business to consolidate or standardize various business capabilities to achieve bottom line business values.

The strategic realignment of application and data architectures cannot be ignored or sidestepped and should not fall victim to costly, risk-prone rewrite efforts or packed replacement projects. We should note that modernization can augment rewrite and COTS strategies by providing a more incremental, risk adverse approach.

Business and IT Architecture Alignment Summarization

We discussed the importance of synchronizing business and IT architecture alignment because when business and IT attempt to move forward with a major initiative that lacks synchronization, the unwanted effects can be significant. Business and IT architecture alignment can be achieved, however, through the combined concepts of rapid response deployments of mini-applications, coupled with core IT architecture modernization. These approaches have been proven to work in practice and provide organizations with alternative pathways to ensure that business investments in IT are refocused on achieving business value in the near-term over the long run. Business professionals must always keep in mind that and business and IT alignment must always be *business* ROI focused.

References

[1] "Chaos Summary 2008: The 10 Laws of Chaos," Standish Group, 2008

[2] "Aligning Technology and Business: Applying Patterns for Legacy Transformation," Howard Hess, IBM Systems Journal, Volume 44 Number 1, 2005
http://www.research.ibm.com/journal/sj/441/hess.pdf

[3] Page 229, "Information Systems Transformation," Ulrich, W. & Newcomb, P., Morgan Kaufmann, 2010

[4] "A Business-Oriented Foundation for Service Orientation," Homann, U., Microsoft Corporation, February 2006

[5] "The Standish Group Report: Chaos," 1995, Standish Group, http://net.educause.edu/ir/library/pdf/NCP08083B.pdf

[6] Page 244, "Information Systems Transformation," Ulrich, W. & Newcomb, P., Morgan Kaufmann, 2010

[7] "Chaos Summary 2008: The 10 Laws of Chaos," Standish Group, 2008

[8] "The Quick Win Team Interview with Juanita Lohmeyer, TELUS Communications," BPM Strategies, Vol. 2 Number 4, Nov. 2006

[9] ibid.

[10] Page 4, "Information Systems Transformation," Ulrich, W. & Newcomb, P., Morgan Kaufmann, 2010

[11] ibid., Chapters 5-14

[12] "Architecture-Driven Modernization: Transforming the Enterprise," Dr. Vitaly Khusidman & William Ulrich, http://www.omg.org/docs/admtf/07-12-01.pdf

[13] "Chaos Summary 2008: The 10 Laws of Chaos," Standish Group, 2008

Five

Business Architecture
in Practice

Reality will not be still.
—Marilyn Ferguson, *The Aquarian Conspiracy*

Previous chapters examined business architecture from a variety of perspectives including the motivations for pursuing a business architecture approach; considering the benefits business architecture can offer; organizing a business architecture practice; and using business architecture to close the business – IT divide. The key issue we have yet to explore is how business architecture can be applied to real life challenges and initiatives. In practice, business architecture is used to address some of the most difficult issues that organizations face. This chapter discusses scenario-based approaches for applying business architecture to address these challenges.

To better understand how business architecture provides value, we need to dig a bit deeper into the nature of the challenges it addresses. People are remarkably adept at solving many problems. Innovations the world has experienced over the last 10 years are plentiful and all around us. But certain kinds of problems remain particularly difficult for people to solve. We previously introduced the concept of the revolving discussion syndrome. Most experienced business professionals have participated in ongoing discussions that continually revisit the same problems without gaining consensus as to how to move forward. This can be very frustrating and often results in decisions to "just do something" in order to break the paralysis. Unfortunately, just as frequently that something is an old tried-and-true approach that ends up failing to deliver.

A Parable

It is common for organizations faced with a complicated problem to find that they struggle to determine how to move toward a consensus-based solution. This situation is often characterized as "analysis paralysis" because it often seems like each piece of analysis leads to the need to do another until at some point the results of one analysis calls into the question the validity of an earlier analysis. At that point the process begins what frequently becomes a never-ending feedback loop that fails to converge on an answer. What is it that triggers these kinds of failures to work toward a common decision? There is a well-known story about a drunkard who has lost his keys that provides some insight into the nature of this problem.

On a dark evening, after a long bout of drinking, a drunkard arrives at his house only to find that he has lost his keys. The drunkard tries to recollect where he last had his keys that evening and heads back to retrace his steps. He is searching for his keys when another man happens upon him and asks him what he is doing. The drunkard recounts his tale of how he had lost his keys. Puzzled the man asks the drunkard "but if you know that you didn't lose your keys here why are you down on your knees beneath the streetlamp here searching?" To which the drunkard replies "because that's where the light is."

Much like the drunkard in this story, organizations typically can identify where they have issues. However, their approach to solving them is often a version of looking "where the light is." It is a sometimes overlooked truth that the tools and frameworks we use to examine issues greatly influence the course of action we choose to pursue. At its best, business architecture provides a way of shining light on aspects of business problems that often are difficult to be able to see with current approaches.

What Makes a Problem Problematic?

There is something about particular kinds of problems that make them difficult to attack. These problems tend to share a few common characteristics:

- Complex tradeoffs
- Unclear interdependencies
- Span of control issues
- Span of communication issues
- Lack of accountability
- Too much information and too little clarity

These kinds of issues are more frequently found in situations where the decision involves knowledge that cuts across organization boundaries. In these situations, it is essential to make use of tools that can help extend the decision-makers span-of-understanding. Business architecture is a toolbox of exactly these kinds of approaches. While there are many different analysis concepts and each organization will need to customize these concepts to fit their own particular situation, there are several common approaches and techniques numerous organizations have applied successfully.

Aspects of a Business Architecture

The business architecture framework we introduced in Chapter 1 provides the pieces for an organization to define an integrated approach to managing organizational initiatives. Because these pieces are a "framework" it is up to each individual organization to evaluate which pieces they want to utilize. This evaluation will typically be driven by topics such as:

- Product market position
- Economic trends
- Cost of capital
- New products

The above topics form a superset of the issues that become the focal point for various business architecture scenarios, which we discuss in more detail later in this chapter. These topics and related scenarios then align to your business architecture framework, which provides the basis for capturing, analyzing and viewing information about your business in a larger variety of ways.

While each organization will likely customize its business architecture framework, this does not mean that each organization has to start from scratch. Starting with the basic conceptual business architecture framework we introduced in Chapter 1 (Figure 1.6), organizations can address a wide variety of challenges that are common across a multitude of industries. We dedicate the remainder of this chapter to reviewing a number of sample scenarios that organizations encounter on a regular basis.

We discuss the analysis and strategies organizations have used to address these scenarios within the context of our business architecture framework, underlying knowledgebase and related business architecture blueprints. The topic oftentimes begins with business capability.

Capability-Based Analysis & Investment

If there has been one single concept that has been most strongly identified with business architecture, that concept would be, without a doubt, the idea of a *capability*. We defined this concept in Chapter 1 as "a particular ability or capacity that a business may possess or exchange to achieve a specific purpose or outcome." Capability has become such a key area of concern because it provides a basis for organizations to more easily understand whether or not an initiative is focused on operational improvements or whether it represents an investment decision.

Most organizations believe that they have relatively formal processes for determining whether or not any investment will be made within their organization. However, in practice many organizational investment decisions are made throughout an organization with relatively little oversight or transparency. While these investments result from a variety of different sources one typical outcome is that organizations possess multiple redundant behaviors. These redundancies can be the result of either mergers or acquisitions or be the result of internally developed behaviors across independent product or market segments.

No matter what the underlying cause of these redundancies, organizations are faced with the option of continuing to fund redundant operating costs and accepting the inconsistency of behavior that typically results, or trying to determine how to invest to be able to streamline the organization and reduce the number of distinct behaviors within a particular business area.

Identifying the capabilities that an organization wants to invest in is the first step. Following up on the various initiatives within the organization to make sure that their internal execution is aligned with those capabilities is the second step. Within every organization there are conflicting demands and priorities. In many cases these conflicts cannot be fully reconciled. When these situations arise, focusing on a capability map which is linked to business strategies and organizational structure can provide organizations with a tool to build consensus around investments, drive business alignment across relevant organizational structures and establish a cohesive roadmap for moving forward that executive steering committees and similar horizontal governance structures can drive forward.

Alignment is the "secret sauce" for an effective organization. The effectively aligned organization:

- Knows where it is going and what it wants want to be, so it can deal with any obstacles it finds along the way
- Treats obstacles as decision points that should be evaluated based upon the organization's goals
- Evaluates how it's portfolio of initiatives support the organization's desired outcome

We will discuss each of the following business architecture scenarios with an eye toward the concept of alignment, a common thread that runs through most business architecture-driven roadmaps. The first scenario, Merger & Acquisition Planning & Deployment, has significant similarities to a number of other scenarios including Operational Cost Reduction and Business Unit Consolidation, the latter of which we have rolled into the merger and acquisition discussion. We therefore, provide more detail in this first scenario while touching on the issues and approaches for a number of the other scenarios.

Merger and Acquisition Planning and Deployment

Companies undergo mergers on a fairly regular basis. The typical merger or acquisition brings one company under the umbrella of another company. This may have a significant impact, such as two banks merging into one, or may be of a lesser impact, such as where a conglomerate brings a related or an even a highly dissimilar company under its wing. In most cases, one company will need to merge redundant operations, financial capabilities, business units and other aspects of the enterprise with the newly acquired entity.

While the decision to execute a merger or acquisition is an executive activity, the evaluation of the viability and related costs of creating a combined entity is essential input to that decision. Once the decision has been made to move forward with the merger, the process of rationalizing the resulting business entity often determines the success or failure of the merger or acquisition. And while failure is not always an absolute, exaggerated operating costs, the inability to align approaches or the inability to align common customers and strategies can haunt an organization for decades.

Consider a property and casualty insurance company that is being merged into a larger entity with many other lines of business. In this case, the organization is certain to find substantial redundancies. These redundancies are likely to exist in areas as disparate as marketing and sales, underwriting and claims handling, and investments and reserves management. One of the most common ways organizations approach these kinds of mergers is to start by identifying all the high-level processes within each of the organizations and to begin making a list of possible redundancies. Just performing this step is a significant amount of work because a given organization has thousands of variations of business processes across various business silos. In addition, the ability to evaluate the alignment of these processes at a micro level is almost bewildering. Yet, the challenge remains.

Identifying the processes and dealing with the different names that organizations use for similar work can greatly slow down the process. At a high level, it is often the case where processes appear to be similar and marked as redundant – only to be unmarked as redundant as the analysis drills deeper and finds differences. At this point the analysis struggles to move forward as it is faced with ever mounting disparities across organizational processes. At this point, alignment teams often follow one of two paths:

1. Paralysis results in arbitrary and limited integration of the organizations
2. An executive decision is made that sets clear boundaries about what will and will not be retained within the combined organization

What makes the difference between the two situations? While the individuals involved certainly impact the result, the major consideration is the "scope of understanding." In other words, if the individuals involved in the evaluation cannot define a framework that allows them to systematically move forward then paralysis will be the outcome. In some cases that framework is in the mind of key individuals which allows them to clearly see where they want the organization to head. But in many cases the framework simply does not exist. Where no framework exists, the amount of information available and the interrelationships between them become too complex for individuals and teams to wrap their minds around. No common blueprint exists to facilitate analysis and alignment.

How does an organization manage to dig itself out of this quagmire? A large financial organization faced exactly this problem. Their solution was to turn to capability analysis. This organization developed capability maps that could be used to facilitate value analysis, process analysis, and strategic alignment techniques. We introduced capabilities and capability maps in Chapter 1. Applying this framework as a baseline, teams were able to aggregate and visualize common processes to facilitate the merger and acquisition delivery cycle.

The first step in applying capability analysis to an organization is developing a list of candidate capabilities. Candidate capabilities are derived in a variety of ways including organizational analysis, value stream (highly aggregated, end-to-end business process) analysis, business process analysis or from industry templates. Organizations starting with process models often find it tempting to just cut through some of the initial steps and adopt the process maps *as* capability maps.

This practice can derail a capability analysis effort because it populates the capability map with a large set of capabilities that haven't been evaluated to specify the *range* of business benefits that they support. Value streams and processes tend to cross capability and organizational boundaries. For example, a claims value stream or end-to-end process can enable a customer address change capability, even though this capability is present in other value streams.

This highlights an important distinction between a process and a capability. A process is a series of activities that makes use of inputs and resources in order to create outputs. The set of inputs and the resulting outputs are relatively fixed as part of the process. Contrast this to a capability which is a behavior which allows a range of outputs to be produced given various combinations of inputs. This is the reason that multiple processes often make use of the same capability. In fact, there is not much point in creating or recognizing a capability within an organization unless that capability is able to support multiple processes.

Figure 5.1 depicts an example of how business capabilities can be mapped at different levels to value streams and decomposed business processes. In this example, business capability level one is mapped to the value stream itself while business capability level two is mapped to a given stage within the value stream. Capability level three is mapped to an enterprise ("ideal") view of the business process that represents a stage of the value stream.

This mapping structure can vary depending on how detailed each level of the capability map is.

When applied to the merger and acquisition scenario, this capability, value stream process mapping approach allows an organization to determine if they have situations where multiple processes can be collapsed and supported by a single internal behavior. Figure 5.1 shows how the sales capability is currently deployed through various processes and provides management with a basis for establishing a value proposition for consolidating variations on current state business processes.

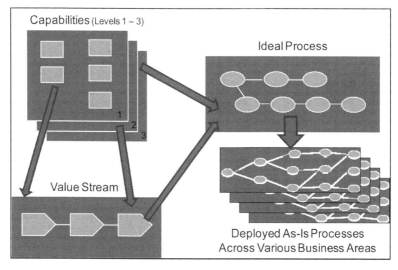

Figure 5.1: Sample Capability, Value Stream,
Business Process Mapping

Value proposition objectives in this example include streamlining customer interactions, shortening the sales cycle and ensuring that the customer views the enterprise with a consistent degree of quality. Other benefits of consolidating capability implementations can retain or improve competitive differentiation, reduce the costs of redundancy and introduce a broader, more flexible set of behaviors that deliver new competitive advantages.

Notice that this is different than the situation where an or-

ganization identifies two separate processes and decides that both
serve the same purpose and that only one will survive. In that case
the organization is identifying that there is no competitive value in
the existing differentiation. At that point, the only question is
which structure is the best one to migrate toward from a one-time
effort standpoint and from an operational standpoint. Regardless
of the approach selected, the business architecture mapping concepts shown in Figure 5.1 support multiple process alignment and
consolidation objectives. Figure 5.2 depicts multiple options for
consolidating business processes that can be applied to the merger
and acquisition scenario.

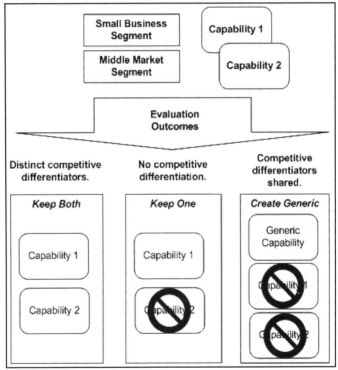

Figure 5.2: Option Scenarios for
Consolidating Business Processes

The capability map does not magically make these decisions

possible. What the capability map does do is provide a framework for approaching the problem that helps organizations have a consistent and visible structure for driving toward these decisions. The capability also facilitates backend business and IT alignment that is often a follow-on set of activities for a merger and acquisition. We discuss the use of capability mapping for business and IT alignment in Chapter 4 and many of these concepts apply to the merger and acquisition scenario.

Figure 5.3 extends the business capability, value stream and process mapping in Figure 5.1 into the IT architecture. In practice, business and IT architecture mapping is often an essential business and IT alignment analysis requirement common to the majority of merger and acquisition initiatives. Mapping business capability and current state business processes to the application architecture provides insights that ensure that business and IT transformation stay aligned as the merger and acquisition strategy unfolds.

Figure 5.3 shows how certain sales related business capabilities have been implemented within two unique applications, each of which originated within a different company under the merger scenario. Capability level two is implemented at the subsystem level while capability level three typically maps to a business service (not shown) within the application architecture. From a business process perspective, we show how a given deployed business process is automated via an interface to an application subsystem. As we discussed in Chapter 4, this mapping, which does not depict the information architecture or desktop shadow systems, facilitates the systematic consolidation of applications as business processes are realigned to support the merger plan.

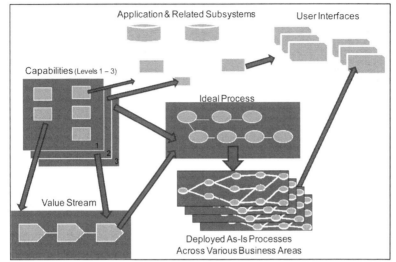

Figure 5.3: Business Capability, Process Mapping
to Current State Application Architecture

Business architecture is suited to merger and acquisition planning and deployment as well as related scenarios such as business unit consolidation, divestiture and operational cost reduction. The remaining scenario discussions provide additional insights into how to apply business architecture in practice.

Infrastructure Investment Analysis

Infrastructure investment and related modernization is one of the most difficult challenges executive teams face. By definition, organizations have infrastructures that were never planned to function in the way they are being used today because infrastructure changes are often deferred due to time, effort and investment requirements. But a growing number of major investment initiatives have triggered a wealth of initiatives that are focused on infrastructure realignment and or directly rely on infrastructure realignment.

For example, more and more organizations have launched

lean value stream initiatives to streamline infrastructure and build new efficiencies into older infrastructures. These value stream efforts are coupled with business process initiatives and new business capability deployment. Most of these projects must be combined with significant IT architecture modernization initiatives. Collectively, organizations are facing a full slate of major initiatives, many of which span multiple years will ultimately impact business infrastructures in a variety of ways. Executives, concerned about the extensive divisional or business unit-driven initiatives are either working at cross-purposes or are attacking similar or interrelated problems in redundant and inefficient ways, are seeking a big picture view of how and if these investments will deliver critical business requirements.

Because infrastructure changes typically require a significant amount of investment and time, a long-term approach is essential to these kinds of efforts. Part of what makes this so difficult is that figuring out what the correct infrastructure should be is a never-ending task. Unless your organization is in a mature and static industry, infrastructure will always lag behind the demands that various initiatives are making on that infrastructure.

When people think about infrastructure something tangible usually comes to mind. Equipment, facilities, communications networks and software platforms are some of the items that most companies would immediately recognize as being elements of their infrastructure. Because investment in these areas have longer-term paybacks it is not possible to manage them solely through the typical initiative-based approaches that focus on determining the cost-benefit ratio and return on investment rates.

This problem is especially difficult for organizations that are not operating in a discrete-manufacturing environment and for projects that involve technology infrastructure. In these situations the organization's infrastructure is more likely to be in a constant state of flux. For many organizations that face this situation that constant state of flux is both an albatross to manage as well as a potential area of competitive advantage and differentiation. These two demands represent conflicting forces pulling against each other. In these situations it is common for organizations to end up in the kind of "analysis paralysis" that was mentioned at the beginning of this chapter.

One insurer faced this problem as the organization began an initiative to rationalize their set of internal software platforms. Their organization had developed a series of platforms over the years each of which served a particular part of their organization's overall process. These systems had been integrated in various ways over the years but the fundamental alignment had remained fairly consistent for at least 10 years. The business now faced some significant change in their marketplace and they identified the need to make parallel changes across these systems as one of the key issues that kept the organization from being able to innovate as fast as some if its peers.

The organization began an evaluation of how it might go about realigning the infrastructure to enable the changes that they saw that they needed. They quickly discovered that several earlier efforts had been made to restructure some of the key software systems that were once again identified as barriers to business innovation. Those previous initiatives had all failed, been abandoned or been restructured to avoid tackling the core issues. In order to avoid repeating the mistakes of the past, the organization commissioned several post-mortem evaluations of these prior projects.

While each project suffered from somewhat different issues what became clear was that all of the projects shared one fundamental issue. The issue they shared was that the initiatives were responsible for delivering "concrete" business benefits. The longer-term strategic realignment of software systems did not deliver these kinds of concrete business benefits. So as the projects lurched forward toward completion, the things that were sacrificed were these long-term benefits. These benefits were considered expendable because they had no direct impact on the project's benefits. Of course the outcomes that were sacrificed were enablers of this longer-term strategic outcome but there was no counter-balancing organizational structure that could advocate for this with any authority.

The organization realized that the core problem that they were facing was how to create a framework that would allow it to manage these kinds of situations. They started by acknowledging that none of the goals was wrong. Each of the goals was driven by a particular stakeholder. The problem was that within the organization there were goals that pulled against each other and the framework that they wanted to construct would have to help guide the choices among these.

To start with, the organization went back to their strategic goals. The first issue that they identified was that the strategic goals were not linked with the processes that they would impact. Because of this they found that it was difficult to define all the potential points of impact that their strategy might have. They decided that each major initiative would be required to identify the process impacts. If any of the processes that those initiatives planned to impact also impacted a process that was linked to a strategic goal then that initiative was required to address how it was addressing the strategic goal.

The assumption was to be that any initiative that impacted a process related to a strategic goal would identify what areas it could address or it could ask for an exception to this approach if it could make a compelling business argument why deferring the strategic goals was an option that should be pursued. This structure put the burden on an initiative to justify any exception to pursuing the strategic goals which provided a level of visibility that the organization previously lacked.

While the organization found that this was a significant improvement, they also found that this alone did not solve their problems. Executives found that if you cannot trace how the pursuit of a strategic objective translates into impacts on specific projects, those objectives will be very difficult to achieve. To address this issue, the organization created a program management linkage to their strategic objectives. Each major program was required to identify how it intersected with any of the outcomes required in order to achieve the enterprise process changes identified. For each of these intersections the programs were required to identify timeframes within which they would achieve those outcomes. Finally, each project within a program was required to identify how it was contributing toward the achievement of the specific program-level outcomes or ask for an exception to allow it not to contribute.

The following example shows how this analysis can be accomplished. Consider that you have three projects (i.e., Projects X, Y and X) deployed across three business units (i.e., A, B and C). Each project is geared at consolidating customer enrollment – which aligns with a major strategic objective for the enterprise. Each project is being driven by a single executive out of a single business unit and, as a result, the teams are taking independent, uncoordinated approaches to meeting this challenge. Collectively, these projects would cost $60 million over a three year window. Executives wanted to take a second look at the viability of this approach.

Information about the business mapped out in the business architecture knowledgebase provided management with increased transparency required to assess this situation. Figure 5.4 shows the conceptual model we used to organize this information in the business architecture knowledgebase. Using the knowledgebase as the vehicle for organizing their analysis, the business architecture team mapped major "in flight" project investments to the customer centricity strategy established at the executive level.

The team further analyzed related funding, business capability impacts and funding analysis to look for related or redundant overlaps and impacts. The team discovered that three unique applications, all of which mapped back to the customer enrollment capability, were being rewritten under projects that could be tied directly back to three different business units.

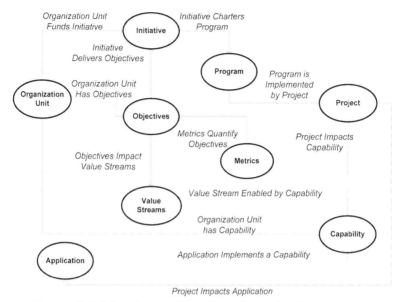

Figure 5.4: Mapping of Enterprise Initiative Investments

Analysis of each project found that there was no cross-business unit collaboration or coordination. The individual projects would still result in poorly aligned enrollment processes, interfaces, desktop systems, applications and databases. The degree of alignment envisioned in the original strategy would not be achieved. As a result, executives asked the three business units to rework their project strategy to align business capabilities, processes and information requirements and to enable a business-driven, IT alignment approach.

This approach achieved a clear alignment of projects with both program level goals and strategic goals. By holding all programs accountable for achieving a commonly coordinated set of strategic goals, the goals were no longer secondary but drove related investments and bottom line results. In addition, through business architecture, the executive team established an effective set of checks and balances to keep the initiative moving forward in a strategically aligned direction.

Shift to Customer Centricity

We have mentioned the desire on the part of numerous organizations to shift to a customer-centric business model. Many organizations today have a product line, business unit or regionally focused business model, which means that as common customer views are multiplied through mergers, acquisitions or just the evolution of your business, a single customer is seen as multiple customers. This occurs even though that single customer sees your organization as a single enterprise. Taking a customer viewpoint can be very difficult for an organization with decades of product line or business unit focused history. Business architecture offers help with achieving customer centricity.

For example, when we followed a customer information management scenario throughout the earlier chapters of this book, we highlighted the fact that a customer should be viewed as a single customer regardless of the business unit or region engaging with that customer. In addition, organizations must understand what the customer owns and all aspects of the relationship with that organization. This is not often the case. Consider the fact that you can go online and get a different and less accurate quote than you may get from a call-in center. Or consider the long distance company that does not know you are also a mobile customer, local customer and a calling card customer. To the long distance provider, there is no connection – which drives customers to leave the company.

The shift to customer centricity must be driven by business executives with explicit objectives and a commitment to make this change. Business architecture provides the visibility to see all of the ways you can engage with a customer, customer focused value streams and enabling processes, the business capabilities that drive change across the business model and into the IT architecture, and the role of customer information that permeates each of these business domains. Business architecture is a vehicle that can be used to achieve customer centricity – *if* an organization commits to such a path.

New Product and Service Rollout

New products and services are the lifeblood of any organization that is competing in a rapidly evolving marketplace. Being able to rapidly innovate is an objective that many organizations are adopting in order to address these demands. But rapid innovation is not something that can just be grafted onto existing practices. Rapid innovation makes tradeoffs between the rate of innovation and the ability to achieve transparency and consistency by having structured repeatable processes.

Improperly implemented, rapid innovation can create something close to process breakdown. This happens when the process innovation invalidates existing oversight and governance structures by failing to conform to their demands. There is truth to the maxim that "process is the enemy of innovation." But if innovation is a key strategic business objective it must learn to coexist with process. What this typically requires is that organizations well-define where process innovation is allowed and where it is not.

One healthcare service provider indicated that they were having trouble reconciling the needs of their organization to beef up their ability to integrate their electronic ordering, fulfillment and servicing services capabilities with the need to create defined and repeatable processes within their business analysis and technology implementation teams. The organization recognized that in their marketplace, time to market was a key competitive advantage. If they did not get their new capabilities to market before key competitors did, they could potentially lose significant numbers of customers that would be very difficult to win back.

Because of the growth within the organization, it was struggling with getting control of a rapidly growing business analysis team that was assisting with the capturing and structuring of requirements to support these projects. This team was struggling to correct the increasing perception that it was one of the key bottle-necks to delivering new service capabilities because it lacked the resources to support the business initiatives. To remedy this problem, the group focused on developing standardized techniques for handling requirements within projects. These standardized techniques allowed new resources to be brought on and to become more effective in less time.

The organization approached the problem by creating a framework that mapped the value elements within the business to customer relationship to processes within the business analysis domain. The organization took the following business architecture facilitated steps to support product rollout.

- Expose all internal organization units, by capability, that are impacted by a new product launch
- Synchronize changes across all impacted processes involved in product deployment
- Ensure that policies, regulations and related impacts are synchronized throughout the rollout process
- Determine impact and synchronize product rollout on backend data and application architectures

This enterprise was able to break through "accepted wisdom" about the role of requirements and end up with an approach where the bulk of new project business analysis work is performed using the newly standardized practices. However, for the web-enablement areas that were identified as key competitive differentiators, a technology-led activity was added to allow the technology team to work directly with stakeholders to speed the identification of valuable new technologies.

New Business Line Introduction

Introducing a new line of business requires coordination across a variety of business lines and IT business units. Consider a scenario where a bank wants to move into a personal lines business, either through expansion or acquisition. Such a move would need to consider where current business units, capabilities, processes and information may be leveraged and where unique infrastructure would need to be established.

This type of assessment and targeted leveraging of existing assets is rarely done. On the contrary, many organizations across a variety of industries have a tendency to clone existing business units, capability and IT environments and then customize these assets to fit the new business. This has typically resulted in a suboptimal solution.

For example, consider the health insurance provider that added a life and disability line to their portfolio. The life and disability lines were driven through existing health insurance business units, business processes, information models, systems and data architectures. This company spent the better part of a decade working around inadequate business processes and missing information, driving up operational costs and driving down policyholder satisfaction. This could have been avoided had this company visualized and integrated the new product line into the business and IT architectures using more systematic approaches.

Business architecture plays an important role in deploying a new line of business. Understanding where current capabilities, organizational units, processes and information can be leveraged in support of this new business unit is the first step. The second step would involve simulating the impact of the introduction of this new line of business on existing infrastructures and determining where that infrastructure needs to be augmented. Finally, the business and IT architecture alignment strategy would be based on visualization and simulation of the projected impacts of this new line of business on business architecture artifacts and corresponding IT architecture artifacts. The business architecture factors that should be considered as part of the new line of business scenario are as follows:

- Business units and capabilities impacted by or that could be leveraged by the new line of business

- Cross-business unit processes requiring modification to support new line of business
- Information to be modified or added to support new line of business
- IT architecture artifacts that need to be updated or added based on business architecture mappings

There are too many moving parts and an overwhelming number of capability and process based redundancies and inconsistencies in enterprises today to continue to deploy new products and services without the visibility that business architecture provides. This healthcare organization was wise in understanding these requirements to streamline product and service deployment.

Streamlining the Supply Chain

Suppliers and business partners engage with multiple business units and roles across a given enterprise. In one case the enterprise may be suffering high costs or discontinuity from a single provider. In the second case, high costs and discontinuity may stem from redundant supplier relationships. This concept includes outsourced business capabilities, which typically result in business blind spots.

Consider a telecommunications firm that uses many sources of customer support services. In one actual situation, a business was contacted six separate times by six separate support centers to say that a services contract had been inadvertently modified. Each unit had access to different records and was apparently using different systems. There was no way to correct this according to the service center representatives. This organization required a map of what was going on with service support centers and business architecture provides such a map.

Extending the visualization of governance structures, including organization units and capability mappings, beyond the walls of the enterprise, creates a virtual view of the business architecture. In the above scenario, a business architecture visualization map would need to be extended to include the customer service capability and all internal and external suppliers that provide this capability.

In addition, the organization should be able to visualize the overlapping or redundant processes, information, products, systems and data that are used by these organization units. Once this new level of transparency has been established, management can develop a roadmap to standardize, streamline and even consolidate these complexities to drive down costs and increase customer service. This information also provides a way to manage the progress of the consolidation process and ensure that an effectively streamlined supply chain management strategy is retained into the future.

Outsourcing a Business Capability

Outsourcing is a business capability enabled initiative. When we introduced the capability map in Chapter 1 (Figure 2.7), we depicted strategic, value add and supporting capabilities. Supporting capabilities vary by industry but examples include human resources, finance, information technology and procurement. Procurement may be viewed as strategic by some industries but is supporting in many other industries. Outsourcing involves handing this capability off to a third party.

Consider, for example, a manufacturing company that wishes to outsource its purchasing capability. This would require management to understand where purchasing is performed. The company will need to determine requirements, move those requirements, processes and related information to an outsourced vendor, and then deactivate those purchasing capabilities within each of the business units performing those capabilities.

Assuming that purchasing is performed in a highly distributed fashion, it may be difficult to see where this should occur without an architectural view of the business. Failure to do so would result in splintered purchasing, replicated capability and high implementation costs. Note that this scenario is tied closely to the concept of business process outsourcing (BPO).

The role of business architecture in this scenario is to provide rapid analysis input into where purchasing is performed organizationally, how processes differ or are the same across business unit silos, which information is used and how IT supports this purchasing environment. In addition, business architecture should support the aggregated views of purchasing and the simulation of what would need to change if purchasing was consolidated into a new, eternal organization unit.

The business architecture related factors that should be considered as part of the business architecture in this scenario include organization units linked to the purchasing capability, processing implementing all purchasing capabilities, the information required to enable a given capability and the mapping between capabilities and process and IT deployments.

Divesting a Line of Business

Divestiture involves taking a line of business and selling it off to another enterprise. For example, consider an insurance company that plans to divest its personal lines unit. All organization units, processes, systems and data structures impacted by such a move would need to be identified so this could be done very systematically. The impacts may not be clear without a map of the business architecture and the ability to visualize what decoupling and divesting a line of business entails and how it impacts various aspects of the business ecosystem.

Divesting a line of business requires identifying all capabilities that support that line of business and making the appropriate changes to the organization units, processes and information to be deactivated. A business architecture map showing these relationships would provide the basis for planning this deactivation effort. In addition, planners could build simulation models to determine the impact or ripple effects on other internal or external organization units.

The business factors that should be considered as part of the business architecture in this scenario include organization units linked to the personal lines related business capabilities, processing enabling those capabilities, related customers tied to the business unit and capabilities being divested, and the IT assets automating related business capabilities and processes.

Change Management

The ability to react effectively and efficiently to changes in external and internal enterprise dynamics is a huge challenge for organizations today. For example, consider the need to respond to a regulatory requirement to engage all suppliers of a given material from certain regions in order to add a surcharge to that material. The impact of such a change would ripple through purchasing, planning, accounting and other business units. It would also impact IT related assets. For a large, diverse organization such a situation would involve major coordination.

The role of business architecture in a change management scenario is to allow managers and analysts to view a living blueprint of the enterprise, drill down into certain aspects such as information related to suppliers and simulate the implications of a change. As change is simulated, impacted lines of business, individuals, processes, information, suppliers and partners, and IT architecture artifacts can be engaged.

The change management scenario requires a drill-down ability to determine specifics of a given change. Drill-down capability indicates the management teams and related personnel that need to be engaged in planning and executing a given change. Key business architecture factors supporting change management include mapping internal and virtual organization units to capabilities and information models, enabling processes and related IT assets. From a change management perspective, being able to do rapid analysis of changes and impacts across a highly transparent business ecosystem provides rapid development of initiative roadmaps that can be rolled out quickly and cost effectively.

Regulatory Compliance

Regulatory issues hit a wide variety of aspects within a given enterprise and the impacts can have ripple effects. For example, a change in a privacy law can impact multiple departments, information models, processes and IT artifacts. Examples included *International Classification of Diseases, Tenth Revision, Clinical Modification* (ICD-10-CM) adoption in the healthcare industry or requirements to move from *Generally Accepted Accounting Principles* (GAAP) to *International Financial Reporting Standards* (IFRS). These are highly invasive regulatory changes that will force organizations to change numerous business domains and IT assets.

These major changes are just one example. Annual regulatory reviews by insurance, banking and other industry regulatory bodies are becoming increasingly sophisticated. In addition by examining end results or asking questions, regulatory bodies are seeking documentation of infrastructures that support the assertions of business professionals to those regulatory bodies. Consider a situation where a federal regulation states that organizations can no longer share a social security number (or similar identifier) with business partners, customers or certain internal business units.

Under this scenario, an enterprise would need to establish a plan, engage relevant business units and partners, identify key documents, change impacted processes and establish a systems impact plan. Many organizations may consider this an IT related issue, but changes of this nature must be coordinated at countless levels across an enterprise. Specific policy aspects of the regulatory requirements must be mapped to various aspects of the organization in order to determine priorities and establish a phased deployment strategy.

Business architecture supports regulatory changes by providing the high-level and drill-down map of impacted aspects and artifacts of the business. An assessment effort would begin with a review of enterprise governance structures, a foundational aspect of business architecture. Business architecture provides the baseline for mapping various policy aspects of the regulatory requirements to impacted organization units, business processes, information and IT assets.

One essential step in addressing such a regulatory compliance initiative would be to engage the relevant and affected parties to address the requirements and changes at a grass roots level. Organization units can engage in collaborative teams that organize around addressing common issues including information impacts and all aspects of the business that fan-out from that information. This requires a widely accessible map of the business that can be updated in real-time by teams across the enterprise as projects are launched and lessons are learned.

Regulatory compliance planning and subsequent deployment projects require mapping and tracking the evolution of the following elements of business architecture and organizational structures linked to business capabilities, supporting information, links from business policies to business capabilities, supporting processes and related IT assets.

Operational Cost Reduction

The operational cost reduction scenario identifies opportunities for streamlining the business. This scenario is characterized by management requests or mandates to find areas within the enterprise where resource spending can be reduced. This may include capability-based realignment, process streamlining, organizational consolidation or a variety of other factors. It also may include user interface inefficiencies that are intertwined with business processes and user-developed shadow systems.

Consider a scenario where there is an operational unit of a telephone company that is responsible for scheduling service calls for commercial and residential customers. The overall business unit is seeking to put a spending ceiling in place. This means that no new people can be hired so the business environment must find a way to cap personnel resources while continuing to support a growth in volume. This scenario is characterized by business-driven, front-line user incremental phases. Each incremental improvement must demonstrate business value. If it does, the solution can be expanded or replicated. If not, it can be replaced with a better approach.

This scenario drills down to a view of the organization unit being targeted for cost reduction to determine the capabilities, related processes, desk top shadow systems and user interfaces being used by those processes. This is a value stream enabled approach that allows executives to envision and drive a phased cost reduction strategy. The planning stage quickly determines the work required to approximate the percentage of cost reduction or cost containment. Ideally, management can run a simulation to project the amount of savings within a given business unit across replicated business units as the situation dictates.

The first level of implementation streamlines processes and concurrently eliminates shadow systems in favor of a new front-end environment. The resulting environment may only be a first level streamlining, where one or more shadow systems are eliminated, or may entail subsequent phases of streamlining. For example, a phase two approach may consolidate backend user interfaces into an automated front-end solution.

The second level of implementation replicates proven solutions into multiple overlapping or redundant business units. In this scenario, this involves replicating the operational solution across other areas that perform the same work, using the same processes. Additional phases of a cost reduction solution rolls up multiple first-cut solutions into more sophisticated, integrated architectures. Business architecture enabled analysis and roadmaps are effective at cost reduction, but allow executives to monitor progress over time.

Globalization

Entering global markets requires the ability to expand the enterprise knowledgebase to incorporate new markets, regions, countries, currencies and other aspects of global expansion. The impact of entering global markets on an enterprise can be very far reaching. Impacts must be anticipated in advance and incorporated into a plan based on the ability of the management team to visualize the cross-functional, cross-disciplinary impacts.

Global transformation is a long-term initiative that takes many forms. It may involve regional expansion into Europe or Asia or may involve a country by country strategy. Each major functional area is likely to feel some impact. This is particularly true when it comes to systems, which may be customized or replicated to address international monetary, regulatory or other requirements. The key requirement for this scenario is to gain rapid visibility into the numerous aspects of the enterprise that are impacted by global expansion, including customers, partners and foreign governments.

Business architecture supports global transformation through the exposure of all business units and external entities that may be impacted by global expansion. This requires full visibility of governance structures, capabilities, information, processes, customers and business partners. Business architecture should also provide the simulation capabilities to determine the impacts of moving into one country, region or continent; shifting to a new currency or metrics environment; or expanding into a worldwide business environment.

Addressing Business Transformation via a Scenario-Driven Approach

Business architecture plays a role in a number of variations on the business scenarios mentioned here, regardless of industry sector or where you are within the lifecycle of that scenario. We have found that it is never too late to introduce transparency and visibility into a given initiative or set of initiatives. If there is a lack of clarity of current or future investments, the Infrastructure Investment Analysis scenario provides insights into how to assess and refocus those investments. While this particular scenario does not prescribe specific actions for reallocating strategic capital from one set of initiatives to another, it offers steering committees and senior portfolio managers a degree of transparency across business unit-based budgeting models that open up new ways in which to evaluate and fund strategic goals and related initiatives.

As information is gathered, populated into the business architecture knowledgebase and exposed to various stakeholders via business blueprints, executives will increasingly come to accept business architecture as a natural step in planning and execution cycles. As your business architecture and stakeholder buy-in matures, you can build more sophisticated simulation of "what if" analysis for various scenarios. Scenarios simply provide a way to structure your information gathering, analysis and resulting discussions around a given set of objectives. As the practice of business architecture and supporting technologies continues to mature, additional scenarios and related ROI models can be expanded to support organizational initiatives.

Six

Getting Started with Business Architecture

All ethics so far evolved rest upon a single premise: that the individual is a member of a community of interdependent parts. His instincts prompt him to compete for his place in that community, but his ethics prompt him also to cooperate (perhaps in order that there may be a place to compete for).
—Aldo Leopold, *The Land Ethic*

In prior chapters, we used commonly encountered scenarios and case studies to demonstrate how business architecture provides enterprise transparency to facilitate issue analysis, resolution planning and funding allocation. With this foundation as a backdrop, this chapter provides guidance on how to launch and sustain your business architecture program. Topics include a discussion on defining your customers, establishing your value proposition, evaluating engagement models, defining the role of technology support for business architecture, evolving the knowledgebase and navigating critical startup stages. We conclude with a walkthrough of the "seven building blocks of business architecture."

Business Architecture Value Proposition

Business architecture offers views of the business that are unavailable from other sources, including IT. Business architecture can tell you what is being done, by which business units, for certain customers, involving various products, via certain processes, involving selected business information. Business architecture generated blueprints serve as the basis for root cause analysis of critical business requirements while providing the foundation for establishing a solution-oriented roadmap that leaves the speculation and guesswork by the roadside. In a word, business architecture delivers "transparency" to a wide variety of internal teams, roles and business units.

The first step in understanding and articulating business architecture's value proposition in your organization is to make sure you clearly understand who your customers are and communicate this effectively. The initial inclination of any senior manager appointed to head up a business architecture team is to assume that their customer is the executive or executive committee that sponsors and funds the team. This is a reality that is difficult, but not impossible, to address.

Revisiting a prior story illustrates a way to address this challenge. A CIO at an insurance company asked one of his executives to launch a business architecture team. The executive's first act, realizing that to be a business architect probably requires actually working in the business, was to request a transfer from IT into the business and the CIO complied. This demonstrates a number of possibilities. A CIO, CTO or head of enterprise architecture are all likely candidates to initiate a business architecture team. IT is a secondary, not primary, customer of business architecture. The executive's move also demonstrates that one individual with the right vision, in this case shifting business architecture into the business, can make a difference when the case is presented properly to the right audience.

The customer issue is front and center when it comes to business architecture and a business focus helps to shape the mission and purpose of the business architecture team. Knowing who your customers are is a basic requirement ensuring that you are maximizing the value of business architecture. From a business perspective, customers include senior executives, program managers, product managers, business managers, strategists and process analysts among others. From an IT perspective, your main customer and partner will be the IT architecture teams – specifically application, data and security architects.

As much as targeting the right customers is important, targeting the wrong customers runs a very real risk of diluting or compromising your value proposition entirely. If, for example, your primary or sole customers are IT application development teams, the value of business architecture will be marginalized to providing incremental improvements to IT projects. If business architecture is not focusing first and foremost on the business as its customer, it is unlikely that it will make a significant difference to the business over the long-term.

One way to identify target customers and clarify your value proposition is to explain how the business architecture team supports and complements existing business teams within the enterprise. This approach not only helps facilitate rollout efforts but allows executive sponsors to understand how business architecture fits into the current infrastructure. An enterprise relies on a variety of standing committees and offices for guidance and governance. These include, for example, executive steering committees, project and portfolio management, planning and transformation teams and various centers of excellence. The following examples are the types of teams that the business architecture team will interact with while delivering value which that team individually could not have achieved on its own:

- Executive Steering Committee
- Business Transformation & Strategic Planning Team
- Portfolio Management Team
- Project Management Office
- Business Process Management Center of Excellence
- Capability-Based Organizational Units

Each of these teams offers unique value propositions to the enterprise. You must, therefore, communicate how business architecture can be aligned within this existing infrastructure. The aspect of business architecture that makes it unique is that it allows other enterprise teams and stakeholders to perform their jobs more effectively by providing visibility of their work within the context of the whole. In addition, work product produced or used by each of these teams can be subsumed by the business architecture, holistically integrated into a cohesive knowledgebase and made available to various teams so that they can each see the whole and not just the parts.

Senior management, in particular, would be able to visualize the cross-functional impacts of various strategies, what it would take to implement those strategies from a roadmap perspective and what work is underway that is related to or in direct conflict with those strategies. Similarly, a portfolio management team would gain visibility not only into projects in progress, but into how each project is tied back to various business strategies, capabilities, organizational units, products and assets. Business architecture is Google Earth to teams and stakeholders across the enterprise. This zoom-in – zoom-out capability is embodied in the business architecture knowledgebase. In turn this provides the business architect with the ability to share and leverage this information across a variety of initiatives and stakeholders.

The most important factor in establishing your value proposition is also where many business architecture teams make their first and potentially most devastating mistake. If you establish your value proposition as previously discussed by targeting the business community as your prime and overriding customer, you will open up opportunities by providing value to a commonly overlooked stakeholder – the business. If, on the other hand, the business architecture team targets IT development teams, business architecture runs a very real risk of being marginalized. This in no way implies that IT does not benefit from business architecture. Rather, IT benefits in ways that are much more profound than what one organization considered their business architects to be – "super business analysts."

There is no better resource or friend to IT than the business architecture team as it opens up a world of transparency into the business that IT may never have even imagined. In particular, the partnership between business architects and IT application and data architects must be particularly strong in order to create the business and IT mappings necessary to bring the full ecosystem into view to support issue analysis, option evaluation and roadmap creation and deployment. As a result, the IT projects that are proposed and deployed are done so with full transparency and understanding of their relationship to the business from a wide variety of perspectives.

The value proposition comes down to asking a simple question. Is business architecture helping the enterprise facilitate strategic planning, address executive priorities, deliver customer value, leverage investments in major initiatives and deploy horizontal solutions across business units? If the answer is yes to these questions, then the business and IT will be well on their way to fully exploiting and leveraging business architecture.

Engagement Models and Deployment Teams

One of the initial challenges business architecture teams will face involves setting up and coordinating teams that work on project-specific or priority-specific initiatives. Business architecture projects differ from traditional initiatives because they often focus on cross-functional, cross-disciplinary analysis, reaching across multiple business units and political boundaries. They require disparate teams and individuals to contribute toward a common objective. The majority of participants in these efforts report into management hierarchies that are separate and distinct from the business architecture team itself. In addition, project timeframes are normally short, placing a premium on the ability to rapidly mobilize participants toward a common purpose and deliverable.

As a result of these unique demands, business architecture engagement models must reflect a more collaborative approach as opposed to a hierarchical approach. While executives may be sponsoring these projects, executing them still requires cooperation from many areas and individuals that do not have business architecture defined in their yearly list of goals. It is, therefore, essential to establish a clear definition of purpose, principles, role definition and governance structure that facilitates a collaborative team approach versus a traditional command and control project governance.

The collaborative governance approach, introduced in Chapter 3, is well suited to the rapid mobilization and execution that is needed to produce business blueprints and roadmaps. Fortunately, extending the collaborative governance structure upon which the business architecture team itself is based can be readily extended to establish engagement models needed for these projects.

To help envision the business architecture engagement model, we will apply it to our customer management consolidation scenario. This initiative is driven by senior business executives working through a Business Steering Committee. The steering committee asked the business architecture team to determine the root cause of slow customer response time customer losses, which was leading to erosion of the customer base. In addition, a second phase of this effort required the team to draft target state options and create a phased roadmap that could be handed off to various business and IT deployment teams.

It has become increasingly apparent to on-the-ground delivery and middle management teams responsible for delivering solutions that those solutions become more viable when the team that must implement them contributes to the overall solution roadmap. Ignoring input and warnings from individuals with frontline responsibilities leads to project roadmaps that are difficult or even impossible to implement. Therefore, business architecture commissioned projects not only need to engage a variety of roles and management levels across business units and technology teams, but must leverage the access that these individuals have with frontline business and IT professionals.

Collaborative engagement models recognize this requirement at the onset of the analysis and planning cycle that spawns these projects. Figure 6.1 provides a template for a collaborative engagement model that steering committees and business architecture teams can employ to reach across lines of business and disciplines to create viable solution roadmaps.

The team structure itself is shown in a series of concentric circles, with the innermost circle containing core team business architects from the Center of Excellence (COE) as well as IT data and application architects appropriate to a given project. The next layer identifies business unit business architects that serve as information gatherers within a given line of business. The outermost circle depicts various analysts and frontline professionals to be engaged on the project. Participation levels decrease for the roles within the outer circles over those roles defined within the inner circles. Collectively, individuals filling these roles form a collaborative team to research a given issue or issues, provide options as to how to address those issues, draft blueprints of the current and target state of the business architecture, and establish roadmaps for various transformations. Projects vary in terms of who is involved based on the issues being considered. Each initiative is driven either directly or indirectly by the executive steering committee or similar executive body.

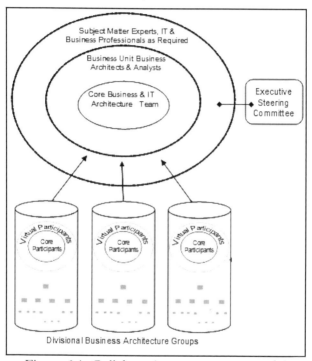

Figure 6.1: Collaborative engagement model
for business architecture assessment work

Deploying an engagement model such as the one in Figure 6.1 relies on having established your business architecture governance structure, as discussed in Chapter 3. The engagement model is an embodiment and an extension of the business architecture team itself. For example, in our customer management consolidation scenario, the steering committee has directed the business architecture team to surface and communicate the factors underlying growing customer dissatisfaction. Such an assessment requires finding and exposing all customer information management "touch points" across each line of business.

Guided by the business capability and organization unit mappings, various business unit analysts and business professionals had to be engaged to determine how customers trigger requests to update contact and related information. Subsequent analysis mapped all business processes that implemented the customer information management value stream. The next level of analysis mapped the findings to relevant aspects of the IT architecture.

This engagement required either having business architects resident in each business unit or establishing that role within each business unit. These business architects excavate the business processes and customer information impacted by those business processes. The core team (at the center of the engagement model in Figure 6.1) then aggregates these processes and information into the customer management value stream, updating the customer information views in the knowledgebase. Process analysts and frontline business professionals support this process but business architects resident within various business units play a key role in information gathering, knowledgebase population and blueprint review and development.

Another aspect of our customer information management example required extending our analysis to incorporate a high-level mapping to the IT architecture. This first level of business and IT architecture mapping required working with the IT architects who formed a part of the core project team. IT application and data architects were incorporated into the core team (i.e., innermost circle) of the project template because they had to be engaged early and often to assess IT related customer touch points, information views of the customer and current automation levels for the customer information management value stream across various lines of business.

As more research was required, the IT architects would reach out to various application and data analysts and experts to derive information about the IT architecture that could be incorporated into the knowledgebase and related blueprints. This completed the analysis cycle and ensured that all parties engaged in the initial analysis effort where required, the degree appropriate, to meet the goals set by the executive committee.

This engagement model may seem unnecessary to the business architecture team that is just starting out, but it helps guide you through initial projects and eases the transition to later stage projects where business architecture teams must scale up to larger, multiple projects. Note that while this engagement model scales up to support large initiatives, it can also be scaled down to accommodate small-to-mid-sized organizations. The template is just a starting point that should be adjusted on a case-by-case basis according to project scope, enterprise scale and organizational alignment. The power of this engagement model is that the core team can magnify its reach and impact, while leveraging business architects, IT architects, business analysts and business professionals across the business.

Roadmap Deployment: Extending the Business and IT Engagement Model

As executives sign off on transformation strategies and roadmaps, the business architecture team cannot simply throw those roadmaps over the wall to IT to implement and walk away. Horizontal initiatives, as our customer consolidation scenario has demonstrated, cannot be solved by IT alone. Rather, business and IT must work as active partners to undertake phased synchronization of business and IT architectures to achieve the business goals set forth by the business executives driving these efforts. The role of business architect in this scenario is that of mentor and advisor throughout the life of a given roadmap deployment.

The challenges and concepts we covered in Chapter 4 regarding the synchronization of business and IT transformation work cannot be achieved merely through improved business and IT architecture mapping. Horizontal initiatives do not lend themselves to a business as usual approach because most IT projects today tend to be silo-based. As a result, executives must consider leveraging a collaborative engagement model that enables silo-based business units to engage with IT as the organization works through initial and later stages of a given roadmap.

Business architects provide transparency into these scenarios. Transparency comes through exposing the overall governance structure within the enterprise and through the ability to collaborate with business teams across business units. Both of these capabilities are essential in initial roadmap stages where even greater collaboration is required. For example, our customer consolidation roadmap called for consolidating customer information management across business unit boundaries. This initiative has a direct impact on the customer information management value stream, all business processes aggregating to this value stream, customer information and views, shadow systems, IT applications and related data structures.

As a result, business and IT should consider various alternative options to the traditional silo-oriented, analysts focused business and IT engagement model. Figure 6.2 depicts a business and IT engagement model that business and IT architecture teams can recommend to executives sponsoring these types of projects. This model is an extension of the social network view of enterprise governance introduced in Chapter 2.

The diagram in Figure 6.2 depicts an insurance company's property and casualty (P&C), life and disability (Life) and health (Health) insurance lines of the business. Each line of business has the capability to sell, administer, bill, process claims and manage customers for their line of business.

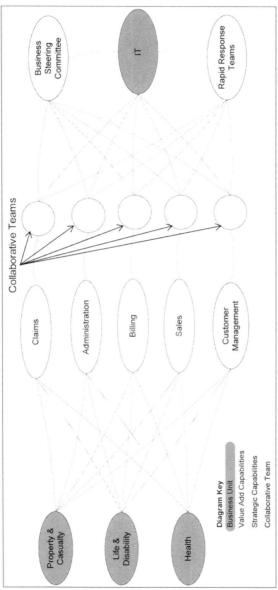

Figure 6.2: Business and IT collaborative engagement
for business-driven IT alignment

The circles to the right of these five business capabilities represent collaborative business teams comprised of individuals from each line of business who are knowledgeable in those particular capabilities. These teams deliver value from a practical perspective, working through issues on a business as usual basis, and also play a key role in business and IT alignment of frontend and backend IT architectures.

The five capability centric, collaborative teams shown in Figure 6.2 discuss and address common business requirements related to their particular capability. These collaborative teams are comprised of business professionals with frontline experience and knowledge of a given capability for their line of business. Issues may focus on addressing standard business challenges such as claim turnaround time. Where automation issues arise, they avoid one-off, shadow system based solutions in favor of more robust, transparent and reusable options.

For example, an administration oriented team may discuss how enrollment issues might be more effectively addressed across P&C, Life and Health lines of business through a more streamlined enrollment process. Their work may trigger automation requirements that may be routed to the appropriate party based on backend IT architectures and cross-capability nature of the issue.

One important point in this engagement model is that the collaborative business teams address business issues and decisions prior to sending them into IT. Over the years, any problem that occurred where a system was remotely involved was thrown over the wall to IT. As a result, backlog requests number in the thousands, many of which are conflicting or confusing as they cross organizational units and capability boundaries. The business wants IT to sort these out, which is not only risky but unlikely to yield any reasonable business value. The collaborative teams can vet issues within the business, ensure that non-IT issues related to process or other business matters are addressed within the business, and deliver a more concise, functionally aligned set of requirements to IT.

As shown in Figure 6.2, the steering committee is a team of

business and IT managers that review cross-functional requests to determine the best way to proceed on any number of more strategic issues. Most organizations already have such a team in place, but additional governance in this scenario dictates specific request types that do and do not get routed to this team. The business architecture team would work closely with this team on situations where horizontal initiatives are considered for business and IT alignment. When a request is deemed to be strategic and crosses business capability lines, that request is routed to the steering committee for consideration.

The steering committee has a higher degree of oversight and perspective than the business systems owner within IT and can review the issues being raised, determine the degree of alignment with top business priorities, request a business architecture based assessment, facilitate roadmap development, procure or allocate funding, and rout issues appropriately.

Figure 6.2 also depicts the "rapid response team" concept. The concept of the rapid response team is based on the principle that any business requirement that has no direct impact on existing application and data architectures may be addressed using highly agile, process-driven solutions. A decision matrix facilitates this analysis further to ensure proper routing and governance. Rapid response solutions provide automation and integration as a stepping stone to evolving larger, more sophisticated backend application architectures. The following concepts describe the ideas behind the rapid response team concept:

1. Small (2-3 people) business and IT team mobilizes around a particular business user and customer issue at the frontline of the business.
2. Initial scope is contained to small, frontline business team where the scope of control and success is very manageable and predictable.
3. The collaborative team is solution oriented, business-driven and ROI focused.
4. Work focuses on concurrent process streamlining, automation

of manual steps and removal or automation of desktop technologies.

5. Additional work can result in elimination of dual entry and
    automated interfacing to cumbersome backend architecture
    user interfaces.

6. Agile principles drive this work, delivering solutions early and
    refining them as required.

7. Initial solutions should be deployed quickly and evolve those
    solutions through iterative feedback from frontline business
    professionals and customers.

8. Reuse of previously deployed services is a key guiding princi-
    ple for the team, contributing over the long-term to a rich
    foundation of business services for future use within the IT
    architecture.

9. After appropriate iterations, the solution is replicated as ap-
    propriate to other areas that have either overlapping or redun-
    dant processes.

10. As a solution matures further, the team seeks opportunities to
    broaden the coverage to upstream or downstream
    processes.

11. This cycle continues until a mature, frontend "mini-
    application" emerges and is deployed to various business pro-
    fessionals who can benefit accordingly.

12. Upon determination by IT and business architects, the mini-
    application is documented according to its perceived longevity
    and handed off to the appropriate IT support
    organization.

13. Multiple teams, working on concurrent solution building ef-
    forts, are governed by a set of guiding principles to ensure
    frontline user participation, design and deployment agility, re-
    use, required funding and appropriate degrees of support.

The rapid response approach should not be confused with
quick fix, middleware solutions that compound convoluted business and IT architectures. Rather, we are suggesting that the fron-

tend of most business-driven roadmaps involves taking small steps that deliver significant business value while bringing improved clarity to later roadmap stages which are likely to take more time and funding. For example, organizations, such as TELUS Communications, using the term "Quick Win," have deployed just such an approach to great success. [1] Figure 6.2 provides the governance structure that can be used to not only establish and leverage rapid response teams, but also provide other avenues of communication and collaboration between business and IT.

The rapid response team approach has been proven to deliver significant business value in practice, while establishing a foundation for subsequent backend IT architecture evolution over the long-term. For example, when these solutions have been deployed across multiple business teams or business units, a de facto set of common semantics emerge from these mini-architectures. Data architecture alignment evolved almost transparently as mini-architectures matured and spread across business units and business capabilities. In addition, these new mini-architectures can, in many cases, become the new building blocks of your backend application architecture, serving as a basis for refactoring and deactivating backend applications and deploying new business services through these new solutions.

The business and IT engagement concepts depicted in Figure 6.2 allow organizations to solve complex, horizontal solutions more effectively and expeditiously. This is accomplished through selective role redefinition, direct business and IT engagement and an agile, rapid response approach that lowers the risks and increases near-term ROI of deployed solutions. The most important factor here is to transform a business and IT engagement model that has been oriented toward silo-based requirements analysis, funding and deployment into one that allows an enterprise to solve horizontal challenges while maximizing the value and contributions of a wide range of business and IT professionals.

Care and Feeding of the
Business Architecture Knowledgebase

We previously introduced and discussed the role of the business architecture knowledgebase and how it enables business architecture analysis, planning and transformative deployments. The business architecture knowledgebase is a means to an end – not an end in itself. The knowledgebase provides a vehicle for capturing, assimilating, viewing and sharing a wide range of information that can be readily transformed into useful business blueprints for business and IT professionals. Most of these professionals, however, will be aware of the knowledgebase only in passing, if at all, and have little interest in knowledgebase structure or management. As long as the knowledgebase serves its purpose, it can and should remain out of the limelight.

Yet there is a small group of business and IT architects who must think about the care and feeding of the knowledgebase and they should base their efforts on best practices, internal requirements and core principles. We have provided some suggested approaches for organizing business domains based on best practices, but it is equally important to temper best practices for what works for your organization. [2] For example, if you want to represent business capabilities to level five, then this must be reflected in the knowledgebase. If your view of a value stream varies or aligns with a particular methodology, this should also be reflected in your knowledgebase.

Terminology used to represent various business domains is also important. If you are a hospital, you have patients, but if you are a government agency you have constituents. Service firms have clients while insurance companies have customers. Internal naming conventions matter as well. If you are broken into divisions and departments, then you use these terms accordingly. If you are aligned based on line of business or groups, these terms should be used.

Agreeing to and adhering to some basic principles can ensure that the knowledgebase will serve its purpose long-term. The following principles can help as you establish and build out your business architecture knowledgebase:

1. A stable baseline metamodel aligns with best practices and internal business requirements.
2. Business value and business blueprint requirements dictate the structure and related investments made in the knowledgebase.
3. Information in the knowledgebase is open and available to all relevant professionals unless it violates security or privacy concerns.
4. The knowledgebase is populated as appropriate to the business value it delivers and related projects it facilitates.
5. Use of technology to support the knowledgebase is appropriate to the maturity of your business architecture efforts.

Establishing, populating and leveraging the knowledgebase require a significant degree of pragmatism. For example, on one government project we used an Access database to represent business units, business capabilities, applications and subsystems. While this was a very high-level mapping analysis, it was incredibly helpful in demonstrating to the executive team that their business and IT mandate had significant implications across multiple business lines and political domains.

One good rule of thumb is to focus on the business, and not on the knowledgebase repository. Focusing on the business professional and the value you can provide ensures that you will not spend too much time on the repository and too little on your target customers. This means that the only information added is the information required for a given assessment or planning effort and additional information is filled in later. On the other hand, it is important to not sidestep the capturing and populating of this information as projects evolve. We have seen repositories that have lagged behind and not evolved. This means that scattered analysis in random drawing tools will not be available for future projects.

Supporting your business architecture knowledgebase requires a degree of commitment and a skill set that would typically reside within the business architecture center of excellence. This is not likely a fulltime role unless you are part of a very large organization, in which case it is more than justified. If you have established your business architecture team within the business (versus within IT), then you may have to obtain repository tool expertise on loan from IT or in conjunction with IT architecture efforts. You also can identify and staff this role internally or externally to the enterprise.

Another issue that arises is the tie between your business architecture knowledgebase and your IT architecture knowledgebase. IT architects typically have an extensive view of the IT architecture with limited line of sight into the business. An excellent opportunity for IT to extend and clarify its view of the business ecosystem by leveraging the business architecture knowledgebase is therefore opened up. From a best practices perspective, the extended business architecture knowledgebase would include basic business and IT domain mappings. These would include mappings among application and capability; process, shadow system and user interface; information and data store; and other extensions as dictated by various analysis and deployment initiatives. Knowledgebase management and IT architecture knowledgebase mapping both tie into the tool discussion in the next section.

The important consideration when assessing the approach, time and investment in establishing and maintaining a knowledgebase is the return on value it provides. Gaining an appreciation of the use of a knowledgebase on an ongoing basis can be achieved through the negative experience associated with restarting every project with a lengthy frontend assessment. Having had to scour through a multitude of disjointed and overlapping business diagrams, spreadsheets and narratives on project after project, one can quickly build an appreciation for having this information in a structured, well aligned and readily accessible knowledgebase.

The bottom line is this. If the knowledgebase is providing

value to business and IT professionals as it evolves and matures, then you have applied the correct set of principles and have created an excellent foundation for future assessment and deployment initiatives.

Technology Tool Guidelines for Business Architecture

On one government assessment project, the analysis team used an Access database to capture and share business and IT architecture mappings with the management team. [3] We do not recommend using this quick and dirty solution as the norm, but it highlights two important points. First, any tool with the ability to create and share a wide variety of relationships across business, and in this case, IT domains can fulfill the most basic business architecture tool requirements. Second, you can perform rudimentary business architecture assessments without making a significant investment in tooling – at least initially.

When considering tool support for business architecture, it is important to remember that the discipline of business architecture is tool-enabled, not tool-centric. However, as your work matures, so do tooling requirements. In the above government example, it would have become onerous to continue using an Access database to expand and mature the business architecture over the long-term. Therefore, you want to begin planning for tool support early in the business architecture deployment cycle.

We recommend that business architecture teams consider a solid technological platform for housing their knowledgebase and providing the business blueprints so essential to the business architecture discipline and the projects that use this information. We have provided basic guidelines to ensure that your technology investments align with your business architecture requirements:

1. Any tool that you plan to use to enable your business architecture efforts should ideally come from a tool vendor that has an understanding and a commitment to supporting business

architecture deployments. If this is the case, many of the other requirements that follow will begin to fall into place.

2. A fundamental requirement for a business architecture tool is that it be based on a customizable metamodel for storing and associating various business and IT domains. This implies that users can easily modify the names and the relationships of the business domains and, where applicable, IT domains within the repository. No matter how well a given vendor prepackages its metamodel to accommodate business architecture, businesses must plan to customize domains and relationships to align with their specific business ecosystem.

3. The tool repository should incorporate a prepackaged business architecture template that contains basic business domains and relationships. So many enterprise architecture tools come with hundreds of IT and business domains, with a heavier focus on IT architecture over business architecture. These enterprise views can be customized, but require a great deal of effort, even if you know what you are doing. However, the implication behind this IT focus is that the vendor lacks an understanding and commitment to support business architecture and this is likely reflected in blueprint availability and a lack of ongoing commitment to support business architecture.

4. Just having a solid underlying repository in which to house your knowledgebase is not enough if you cannot provide a variety of views of that information to business professionals to support analysis, planning and deployment initiatives. A tool should also include prepackaged blueprints and flexible reporting. Customers should expect that a tool provides a core set of blueprints, but they should also have confidence that a vendor is continuously working on expanding those core reporting requirements. A basic set of blueprint reporting should include the ability to generate:

    - Canned and ad hoc business domain cross-reference reports
    - Extended cross-reference reports that represent business

and IT domain mappings
- Capability maps and heat maps
- Value stream representations
- Value stream and business process decomposition and aggregation views
- Organizational diagrams, preferably in the form of social networking or similar diagrams

In addition to the above requirements, vendors should be considering support for additional blueprints such as the balance scorecard. In addition, tools should have the ability to either store or link to related blueprints. For example, if you follow a repository path to decompose a value stream into a process and then decompose that process to the next level process, the repository should have the ability to store and allow you to view processes at any level. A fallback option is the ability to link from the repository to externally stored views of that business process.

5. Another important requirement is ease of use and access of the repository. The process of populating information into the knowledgebase should include manual options and automated interface options. A related feature is viewing (versus updating) capabilities over the Web. While a small number of professionals will control the population of the knowledgebase, many individuals should and will require access to the information within the knowledgebase. Therefore, there should be a facility for Web-based browsing, inquiry and reporting.

6. Finally, the vendor you choose should participate in and stay current with the latest set of evolving standards in business architecture. Whether this means aligning the tool with basic metamodel views, tool interchange standards or blueprint perspectives, vendors should be cognizant and engaged as these standards evolve. This also means that business architecture vendors should stay active in various standards groups to both influence and benefit from those standards – which in turn are

reflective of best industry practices. A vendor that does not acknowledge or participate in the work of the standards community must be viewed with a degree of suspicion because this means that it is evolving its tools based on its own view of the solution.

The depth of mapping required between the business architecture and IT architecture and use of the knowledgebase by IT increases the breadth of knowledgebase domains and tool integration requirements. Tool integration capabilities can ensure that in depth IT architecture knowledge can be continuously aligned to the business architecture. In solutions previously recommended, requirements focus on standardized blueprints and metamodels, ease of use, integration and general accessibility, thereby reducing the amount of time and investment in repository management.

However, there is still a degree of knowledge and commitment required when establishing and utilizing a business architecture knowledgebase within a tool. Consider that if you do not make this commitment, the time, effort and risks associated with project-by-project analysis of disjointed diagrams, spreadsheets and narratives will increase exponentially over the baseline investment in the tool and related knowledgebase.

Seven Building Blocks of Business Architecture

We close our discussion by leaving you with the seven building blocks of business architecture. These building blocks summarize and reinforce what we have been discussing since Chapter 1 and provide a quick way for communicating your business architecture strategy and rollout topics. We do not want to imply that there is a strict step-by-step progression associated with the seven building blocks, but each topic area does build upon previous topic areas. Figure 6.3 depicts a view of the seven building blocks, beginning with determining objectives and moving through the concept of continuous refinement.

Figure 6.3: Seven Building Blocks of Business Architecture

The basic building block involves understanding your business objectives and owner and engagement concepts. While several of these tasks will be ongoing, understanding what you want to accomplish from a business architecture perspective is a top priority. This will have a direct bearing on governance and engagement models within the enterprise. Consider, for example, that your main objective is to deliver business value to your executive strategy and transformation committee. Your reporting structure must reflect this objective. If your center of excellence reports to the head of enterprise architecture, who in turn reports to the CIO, then you will never even begin to satisfy this objective.

Objectives and governance reporting also impact engagement models. If the center of excellence is under the IT organization, then an engagement model must be created to engage the business on business architecture. We discussed the business and IT engagement model earlier in this chapter and IT attempting to push business architecture on the business without the business gaining a sense of ownership repaves many of the paths that IT has been attempting to plough for years. However, if business architecture is centralized outside of IT, then the engagement model shifts toward the structure we introduced in Chapter 3.

Another step within this foundational building block involves determining how you and the executives you report to plan to evaluate ongoing contributions to the enterprise. This can only be demonstrated through practice but should be tied to a clear set of objectives within this early stage of the business architecture life-cycle. The value proposition discussion at the beginning of this chapter provides guidance into this area.

Motivation and intent, driven by business architecture objectives, will carry a significant influence into your deployment work and should be considered carefully at the outset. This is the reason for incorporating objective setting, governance and engagement model topics as the foundation of the seven building blocks. A natural outgrowth of the objective setting and governance discussion is expanding the overall team structure through many of the governance topics we covered in Chapter 3. This building block solidifies team structure, virtual relationships with business unit business architecture and IT architects. It also serves as the point where you will be solidifying your engagement model in practice as initial projects begin to take shape.

Building block three brings the knowledgebase into the picture. Establishing and maturing the knowledgebase is an ongoing task but putting a baseline knowledgebase in place should be a team priority as you move from building block two up through four. This may not necessarily involve tool selection and procurement, but knowledgebase deployment will need to address your technology options and plans.

Building block four, identifying top business priorities, goes hand in hand with building block five, initiating projects. Project selection should have a direct relationship to the critical business issues that the business is facing. Initial efforts should be of a nature where the team can demonstrate value in a period of days or weeks – not months. Tell management something that they do not know that impacts planning and decision making around a priority issue. For example, tell them why you are losing customers or where redundantly deployed capabilities across business units are driving up operational costs.

The aspect of building block five is that it provides the opportunity to begin to mature the content of the knowledgebase.

This is why it is important to establish the knowledgebase in building block three. As we have stated before, the knowledgebase is populated incrementally with each project adding more information to the baseline. Early projects will have to gather more information than later projects, but as the knowledgebase matures, project teams will go to it again and again as it becomes a central reservoir of knowledge about the business and about how the business leverages and interacts with IT deployments.

Building blocks four and five also have the added value of expanding and solidifying engagement models, which takes us to building block six. There are different types of engagement models as we discussed earlier in this chapter. One type of engagement model addresses the assessment work that is ongoing within the world of business architecture. A second type of engagement model addresses ongoing deployment. We added this to the discussion in this chapter because the entire concept of business engaging in and driving initiatives may be new and different for many organizations, particularly if IT has taken over this role in recent years. This second type of engagement model is unlikely to begin to mature to any degree until this later stage building block.

Finally, building block number seven moves us toward a goal that most organizations should strive to achieve: continuous synchronization. This is business architecture's version of Nirvana. At this stage, organizations will have dramatically reduced the painful, costly and high risk start and stop initiatives that have come to characterize business funding models in favor of continuous, short-term, low risk, high payback business and IT alignment efforts. While this may be difficult for business executives to envision, following the guidelines we have set forth in this book will take you a long way to achieving this vision.

References

[1] "The Quick Win Team Interview with Juanita Lohmeyer, TELUS Communications," BPM Strategies, Volume 2 Number 4, Nov. 2006, http://www.bpminstitute.org/uploads/media/UlrichQA_01.pdf

[2] Sample Business Architecture Metamodel, http://www.omgwiki.org/bawg/doku.php?id=businessarchitectur eitalignmentmapping

[3] Pages 228-230, "Information Systems Transformation," W. Ulrich / P. Newcomb, Morgan Kaufmann Elsevier, 2010

Index

A

abstractions 46, 49, 63
aggregation 49
Airbus (A380) 32
alignment 55
analysis paralysis 163, 176
application architecture 55, 133
application systems 52
architecture knowledgebase
.... 46
audit 135

B

Balanced Scorecard 53
baseline data 71
best practices 91
blueprint 31, 37, 63, 136, 187, 195, 210
Bohm, David 61
business analyst 95
business and IT alignment 56, 144
business and IT architecture
.... 145, 159
business architect 92, 96, 119
business architecture ... 39, 44, 48, 72, 117, 133, 163, 165
business architecture
(defined) 30
Business Architecture COE

.... 104, 111, 117
business architecture
dashboard 73, 76
business architecture
framework 76, 81
business architecture
knowledgebase 57, 78, 143, 178, 210
business architecture team 22, 27, 30, 40, 41, 59, 86, 91, 95, 100, 102, 106, 117, 178, 195, 196, 198, 199, 200
business benefits 129, 176
business capabilities 48
business ecosystem 186
business performance 54
business process
management (BPM) 132
business process outsourcing
(BPO) 186
business process vs.
capability 170
business processes 52, 147, 173
business rules 46
business transformation 55, 146
business visualization 52

C

capabilities 68, 82, 210

capability map...... 52, 83, 172
capability mapping........... 184
capacity 166
center of excellence 91, 96
change management 187
Chevron............................ 64
Chief Information Officer
    (CIO) 98
city planning....................... 34
client facing capabilities..... 54
Cloud Computing 38, 130
collaboration 96, 105, 111,
    209
collaborative governance 114,
    117
collaborative teams 54, 152
command and control...... 96,
    117
commercial-off-the-shelf
    (COTS)......................... 144
competitive value 172
compliance 54, 135
cross-functional
    collaboration................ 115
cross-functional team 105
current state 56, 141, 146
customer centricity........... 180
customer focused value
    streams 180
customer information
    management 180
customer integration........ 127
customer satisfaction 77
customer service capability
    185

Cutter Research...................39

D

dashboard 70, 73, 80
data architecture......... 55, 133
data management............. 135
decision matrix................. 207
decision points 167
decision-makers span-of-
    understanding 165
decisions...............................72
decomposition.....................49
divesting a line of business
    186
divisional knowledgebas . 111
drill down............................71

E

ecosystem............................54
end-to-end business process
    ....50, 170
engagement model... 201, 219
enterprise architecture.......55,
    100
*Enterprise Architecture as
    Strategy* 44
enterprise complexity.........30
enterprise ecosystem 42
enterprise service bus. 44, 99,
    126
ERP systems........................67
executive steering committee
    108

F

federated knowledgebase 111

Ferguson, Marilyn 161
fragmentation of
   management viewpoints 53
framework 57, 165
Free Floating Business
   Architect.......................103
future state 56, 146

G

GE..19
global markets...................191
global transformation 191
governance 77, 81, 91, 209

H

heat maps 215
Homann, Ulrich 144
horseshoe 156
how...............................48, 72
Hyatt Regency Crown
   Center 65

I

IBM 29
implementation........ 109, 190
information mappings 84
information overload.........63
infrastructure investment 174
insight................................63
IT architecture 44, 52, 55,
   107, 124, 126, 133, 137,
   145, 180, 203, 208
IT costs 78
IT investments..................129
IT silos 149
IT stewardship..................136

IT transformation 173
IT-driven solutions.......... 129

K

knowledgebase 43, 76, 111,
   141, 211, 219

L

Leopold, Aldo 193

M

mentor 203
merger or acquisition 168
metrics 80, 82
middle management 200
modernization 155
modernization projects ... 151
monitoring techniques 68
multi-enterprise business
   architectures 47
multi-enterprise ecosystem 47
multi-project, multi-year
   initiatives..........................70
multi-year projects 37

N

new line of business
   introduction.................. 182
new product and service
   rollouts 181

O

operational cost reduction
   189
operational improvement ..87
operational metrics 69, 70

organizational structure... 117
outsourcing 185
over the wall.................... 206

P

parallel changes................ 176
perspectives...................... 49
phased deployment.......... 149
policies 46
Porter Value Chain 53
portfolio managers............ 30
principles for a Business
      Architecture COE 118
process innovation........... 181

Q

quick and dirty solution... 213
Quick Win........................ 153

R

rapid innovation 181
rapid mobilization 199
rapid response.......... 207, 208
realignment...................... 189
redundancy....... 127, 140, 171
refactor 109
refactoring....................... 158
regulations 46
regulatory compliance 188
repository 214
ripple effects 187
roadmap............. 86, 146, 203
ROI models 192
role definition 117
root cause analysis........ 19, 86

S

scenario-driven initiatives ..76
scenarios.............57, 172, 192
seven building blocks of
      business architecture... 216
shadow systems 133, 136, 190
silo-based solution.............76
small-to-mid-sized
      organizations................ 203
SOA............................ 38, 130
social network diagram 53, 84
social networking............. 117
Standish Group.......... 38, 152
strategic goal.................... 177
strategic initiatives 87
streamlining.............. 189, 190
structural limitations...........82
suppliers and business
      partners 184
supply chain management
      53,185
supporting capabilities 185

T

tactical............................ 46, 5
technical architecture 55, 134
TELUS Communications
      .... 153, 209
The Land Ethic.................. 193
The Lives of a Cell...............89
Thomas, Lewis...................89
Titanic..............................27
touch points.............. 56, 202
transformation 145
transformation initiatives 133

transparency 42, 63, 70, 78, 98, 101, 111, 115, 125, 153, 185, 192

U

Unified Modeling Language (UML) 45, 137

V

value propositions ... 171, 198
value stream 50, 82, 141, 153, 190, 202
value-focused investment analysis 68
viewpoints 80
virtual enterprise 53
virtual participants 108

visibility 63, 72
vision 46
visualization 83

W

Watts Humphrey 57
Web 2.0 136
Web-based 215
what 48, 72
where 72
who 48
why 48, 72

Z

Zen and Creative Management 121
zoom-in / zoom-out 49

About the Authors

WILLIAM ULRICH is President of TSG, Inc. and management consultant specializing in business architecture and business and IT alignment. Ulrich has worked with hundreds of large corporations and government agencies over his 30 plus year career. This is his fifth book with his last publication being *Information Systems Transformation* (2010). Ulrich is Co-founder of the Business Architecture Guild, Co-chair of the OMG Business Architecture Special Interest Group and OMG Architecture-Driven Modernization Task Force, Editorial Director of the Business Architecture Institute and member of the Penn State Enterprise Architecture Advisory Group. Ulrich is also a Cutter Consortium Senior Consultant. He travels, publishes and speaks extensively and is based in Northern California.

NEAL MCWHORTER is a Principal with Enterprise Agility and helps organizations improve their ability to deliver new business capabilities and business applications through the use of Business Architecture, Business Process and Business Rules techniques. As a frequent presenter at industry conferences, he has authored numerous white papers and articles in the areas of business architecture, business process analysis and business rules management. He provides mentoring and leadership services to Fortune 1000 clients in the areas of requirements analysis, rules-driven business process management and business process transformation. McWhorter is Co-founder of the Business Architecture Guild and co-chairs the OMG Business Architecture Special Interest Group.

Get involved ...

Business Architecture Guild

www.businessarchitectureguild.org

Please look around our website to find out more about business architecture, *The Business Architecture Handbook*, our goals for the Business Architecture Guild and why the Business Architecture Guild is the source for an industry body of knowledge.

The Business Architecture Handbook: Body of Knowledge was assembled by the Business Architecture Guild. We anticipate its release in the early part of 2011. We look forward to receiving feedback on this Handbook with a focus and intent on evolving best practices as the industry continues to mature.

Business architecture is changing how organizations implement strategies and transform their enterprises. As organizations move forward into the complex, challenging world ahead, business architecture is leading the way. Business architecture sheds light on complex challenges and solutions by introducing a degree of visibility that did not exist in the past. In doing so, strategic decisions and investments can be made with more confidence, deliver more effective results and do so with less investment than what is currently being spent on major initiatives today. As practitioners of business architecture, with many years of collective experience in the field, we saw the need for a practical guide for the business architect. We have created a comprehensive, yet user-friendly handbook, that focuses on practitioners of the important and growing discipline of business architecture.

Welcome to the Business Architecture Guild
For more info contact info@businessarchitectureguild.org

Get involved ...

Business Architecture Special Interest Group of the Object Management Group

http://bawg.omg.org

Our Mission Statement

Promote industry consensus and
develop a set of standards to support the concept of building,
evolving and aligning business blueprints.

What is Business Architecture?

A blueprint of the enterprise that provides
a common understanding of the organization and
is used to align strategic objectives and tactical demands.

Business Architecture Charter

Business Architecture SIG Charter

Architecture Ecology Charter

Architecture Ecology SIG Charter

Business Architecture Overview

Business Architecture
maps and documents
the essence of the enterprise.

Companion Book

DOT.CLOUD

The 21st Century
Business Platform

PETER FINGAR

ww.mkpress.com/cloud

Watch for forthcoming titles.

Innovation at the Intersection of Business and Technology
www.mkpress.com

Meghan-Kiffer Press
www.mkpress.com